OLD COMEDY AND THE IAMBOGRAPHIC TRADITION

American Philological Association
American Classical Studies

The Harmonics of Nicomachus and the Pythagorean Tradition	Flora R. Levin
The Etymology and the Usage of ΠΕΙΡΑΡ in Early Greek Poetry	Ann L. T. Bergren
Two Studies in Roman Nomenclature	D.R. Shackleton Bailey
The Latin Particle Quidem	J. Solodow
On the Hymn to Zeus in Aeschylus' Agamemnon	Peter M. Smith
The Andromache of Euripides	Paul David Kovacs
A Commentary on the Vita Hadriani in the Historia Augusta	Herbert W. Benario
Creation and Salvation in Ancient Orphism	Larry J. Alderink
Eros Sophistes: Ancient Novelists at Play	Graham Anderson
Ancient Philosophy and Grammar: The Syntax of Apollonius Dyscolus	David Blank
Autonomia: Its Genesis and Early History	Martin Ostwald
Language and Metre: Resolution, Porson's Bridge, and Their Prosodic Basis	A. M. Devine
Descent from Heaven: Images of Dew in Greek Poetry and Religion	Deborah Boedeker
Iamblichus and the Theory of the Vehicle of the Soul	John F. Finamore
Epicurus on the Swerve and Voluntary Action	Walter G. Englert
Seneca's Anapaests	John G. Fitch
Xoana and the Origins of Greek Sculpture	A. A. Donohue
ΑΝΑΓΚΗ in Thucydides	Martin Ostwald
Old Comedy and the Iambographic Tadition	Ralph M. Rosen

Ralph M. Rosen

OLD COMEDY AND THE IAMBOGRAPHIC TRADITION

Scholars Press
Atlanta, Georgia

OLD COMEDY AND THE IAMBOGRAPHIC TRADITION

Ralph M. Rosen

© 1988
The American Philological Association

Library of Congress Cataloging in Publication Data
Rosen, Ralph Mark.
  Old comedy and the iambographic tradition / Ralph M. Rosen.
    p. cm. -- (American classical studies ; 19)
  Bibliography: p.
  Includes indexes.
  ISBN 978-1-55540-305-8

  1. Greek drama (Comedy)--History anbd criticism. 2. Iambic poetry,
Greek--History and criticism. 3. Invective in literature.
4. Cratinus, d. ca. 420 B.C.--Criticism and interpretation.
5. Aristophanes. Knights. II. Title. II. Series: American
classical studies ; no. 19.
PA3161.R67   1988
882'.01'09--dc19   88-33324

Printed in the United States of America

In Memoriam
Nathan Dane II

TABLE OF CONTENTS

Preface		vii
Abbreviations		ix
Chapter I:	Introduction	1
Chapter II:	Iambos and Old Comedy	9
Chapter III:	Cratinus	37
Chapter IV:	Comic Poet and Κωμῳδούμενος: Aristophanes' *Equites*	59
Epilogue		83
Bibliography of Works Cited		85
Index Locorum		91
Index of Selected Greek Words		97
General Index		101

PREFACE

This book is a thoroughly revised and largely rewritten version of my 1983 doctoral dissertation at Harvard University. Though the members of my dissertation committee — Albert Henrichs, Gregory Nagy and Jeffrey Rusten — have not been intimately involved with the revisions, I would like to reiterate here the thanks that I recorded to them five years ago for their scholarly guidance and encouragement.

I am most grateful to my colleagues in the Department of Classical Studies at the University of Pennsylvania for relieving me of teaching duties during the Spring term of 1988, during which time I was able to complete this book. In particular, I thank Joseph Farrell and Peter Bing, who read the entire manuscript in an earlier stage and offered many acute criticisms, suggestions and instructive ψόγοι. For the preparation of the final manuscript I owe my greatest thanks to another colleague, James J. O'Donnell, who contributed time and computer expertise in the production of the laser-printed copy. I wish to thank also my graduate research assistant, Robert J. Gorman, who spent many hours diligently proofreading and compiling the *Indices*. His vigilance saved me from many errors and infelicities, though, naturally, I alone am responsible for those that remain.

Finally, I am extremely grateful to Ludwig Koenen, the editor of this series, for his many detailed and insightful comments on the original draft of the manuscript. Under his learned eye this book has been greatly improved at every turn.

ABBREVIATIONS

Dg = E. Degani, *Hipponactis Fragmenta et Testmonia* (Stuttgart 1983).

Kassel-Austin (KA) = R. Kassel and C. Austin, *Poetae Comici Graeci* (Berlin [vol. IV] 1983, [vol III.2] 1984, [vol. VI] 1986).

Kock (K) = T. Kock, *Comicorum Atticorum Fragmenta* 3 vols. (Leipzig 1880-88).

Koster = W. J. W. Koster, *Scholia in Aristophanem IA: Prolegomena de Comoedia* (Groningen 1975).

Meineke = A. Meineke, *Fragmenta Comicorum Graecorum* 5 vols. (Berlin 1839-57).

W = M.L. West, *Iambi et Elegi Graeci* vols. I and II (Oxford 1971, 1972).

Quotations from Aristophanes are from V. Coulon's Budé edition (5 vols., Paris 1923-30) unless otherwise noted.

CHAPTER I
INTRODUCTION

The comic dramatist of fifth-century Athens composed in a genre that embraced diverse literary elements, each with its own history and conventions. The element that most often came to characterize the genre, personal abuse or, to use the term of Hellenistic scholars, κωμῳδεῖν ὀνομαστί, is no exception.[1] Aristotle recognized this when he referred to the invective, combative aspect of Old Comedy at *Poet.* 1449b8 as an ἰαμβικὴ ἰδέα. There he explicitly traced the invective of Old Comedy to the iambographic tradition: comedy arose from the tradition of poets who "originally made poems of abuse" (πρῶτον ψόγους ποιοῦντες, 1448b27), and in the fifth century poets with such instincts turned to comic drama rather than iamboi (...οἱ μὲν ἀντὶ τῶν ἰάμβων κωμῳδοποιοὶ ἐγένοντο, 1449a3). Aristotle had in mind, of course, the kind of poetry that was best represented for him (as it is for us) by Archilochus and Hipponax. Although these two poets had quite different styles, they were similar in several crucial respects: both engaged in personal abuse against individuals whom they presented as ἐχθροί; both freely employed obscenity (Aristotle's αἰσχρολογία, cf. *EN* 1128a23), verbal violence and humor; both seem to have used quarrels with specific enemies as a poetic leitmotif. All of these literary features are also found in most comic dramatists of fifth-century Athens, and it is generally held, as Aristotle realized, that the ψόγος of the Ionian iambic poet was a direct literary ancestor of the ψόγος of Old Comedy.[2] But while all students of Old Comedy acknowledge the affinity between the two genres, they do so only casually and no one has yet fully appreciated the implications such an affinity has for our understanding of the comic ψόγος.[3] It is perhaps true, as West states, that "in the last resort ... it

---

[1] Plato *Resp.* 395e7, discussing whether the ideal polis should allow tragedy and comedy, and what type of mimesis is most suitable for the guardians, sums up the essence of Old Comedy as follows: οὐδέ γε ἄνδρας κακούς, ὡς ἔοικεν, δειλούς τε καὶ τὰ ἐναντία πράττοντας ὧν νυνδὴ εἴπομεν, κακηγοροῦντάς τε καὶ κωμῳδοῦντας ἀλλήλους καὶ αἰσχρολογοῦντας. At *Legg.* 935d, he speaks of comedy's "zeal for ridiculing individuals" (τὴν τῶν κωμῳδῶν προθυμίαν τοῦ γελοῖα εἰς τοὺς ἀνθρώπους λέγειν).

[2] See, for example, Gerhard (1913) 1904.

[3] Henderson (1975) 2-29, has done much to emphasize the affinity, but he was not concerned to trace in any detail the generic relationship between the two.

remains impossible to define the exact historical relationship of the genres."[4] But there is much that our texts can still reveal about the influence of the iambos on comic drama, even if they do not always allow us to specify exactly when and how iambographic elements found their way into Old Comedy.

In Chapters II and III below, therefore, I shall attempt to show that the comic ψόγος is structurally and functionally similar to the iambic ψόγος, by which I mean 1) that both genres employ similar modes of diction, poetic devices and motifs, and 2) that the goal of each is, in its essential poetic impulse, the same. Moreover, I shall argue that the comic poets, beginning with Cratinus, were conscious of the iambographic provenance of their invective, and that they shaped their poetic attacks according to certain inherited generic conventions. Such an approach has important ramifications for our understanding of comic attacks in the fifth century, since it compels us to examine the influence of literary convention on the poet's acrimonious stance against his targets.

I have chosen to focus such an examination in the fourth chapter on the problematic relationship between Aristophanes and Cleon, especially as it is portrayed in *Equites*. This play provides an exemplary testcase for my argument, since it is nearly always felt to reflect a *historical* quarrel rather than a fictitious one, invented by the poet in accordance with the generic requirements of Old Comedy. While scholars may be ready to admit that Aristophanes' treatment of Socrates in *Nubes*, for example, was conventional, his attacks on Cleon (in whatever plays) are seen to be different, if only because they seem to be more heartfelt and personal. The most telling allusions to Cleon in *Acharnenses* come from Dicaeopolis who, it is often alleged, acts as a virtual spokesman for the views of Aristophanes, while those in *Equites* and *Nubes* occur in parabatic passages, where the chorus often seems to speak on behalf of the poet. On the basis of these passages (together with notices about *Babylonii*)[5] the quarrel has been "historically" reconstructed in some detail. Cleon, it is said, prosecuted Aristophanes in court for having denigrated Athens in the presence of foreigners in 426, and *Equites*, produced in 424, was, at least in part, a response to this prosecution.

The case of Cleon and Aristophanes is indeed curious. By now scholars have been sufficiently admonished not to rely solely on the words of a poet, especially a comic poet, for historical information.[6] Yet,

---

[4] West (1974) 37.

[5] See below, p. 63, n. 10.

[6] In general, see Lefkowitz (1982) xviii-ix; for Aristophanes, cf. Gomme (1962) 70-91, and Chapman (1978) 59-70.

although it is often acknowledged that the evidence for a relationship between Aristophanes and Cleon derives ultimately from the plays,[7] the historicity of a feud between the two has never been questioned.[8] In Chapter IV, therefore, I shall reconsider thoroughly the alleged quarrel in the light of my earlier assessment of the relationship between the iambographic and the comic ψόγος. This is not only because the evidence about Aristophanes and Cleon is dubious — this much is well known — but, more importantly, because scholars have traditionally failed to view the quarrel in the context of the comic ψόγος as a poetic genre. I shall argue that Aristophanes' attacks against Cleon can be viewed as an elaborate literary conceit with direct antecedents in the iambic ψόγος, and that the invective against Cleon in *Equites* in particular must be seen, to a great degree, as conventional.[9] The comic poet, as we shall see, was aware that he was working in a tradition inherited in many repects from the iambos, a genre which had developed its own distinct poetic means of presenting the relationship between poet and ἐχθρός.

A few methodological remarks are here in order. I use the term "iambos" to indicate a poetic genre, distinguished by content[10] rather than meter, although, as the word implies, most iamboi were composed in iambics.[11] Much iambic poetry will not belong strictly speaking to the iambos, such as the tragic trimeter, or the bulk of Solon's iambic verse.[12] The content of the iambos could be quite varied, and not all the surviving fragments are ψόγοι.[13] But in antiquity, as we shall see below, the term "iambos" most often referred to poetry of invective, and implied the presence of literary elements appropriate to this type of genre, such

---

[7] Gelzer (1970) 1399; Lefkowitz (1982) 109.

[8] Halliwell (1984a), 83-88, does not specifically address the evidence for a quarrel between Aristophanes and Cleon, but his remarks, p. 84, are most applicable: "satirical humour is consistently translated in the scholia into objective truth about political or social events, personal appearance, or individual character and behaviour. Above all, it is assumed, with a fine disregard for circularity, that different comic passages with similar satirical content confirm the truth of one another."

[9] When I speak of *Equites* as a "conventional ψόγος" I mean that Aristophanes crafted his invective in accordance with certain distinguishable poetic elements characteristic of the Ionian iambic ψόγος, which had become important literary "conventions" of the comic dramatist engaged in a similar poetic activity.

[10] On the classification of ancient genres in terms of their content, cf. Cairns (1972) 6. On the iambos, cf. West (1974) 22-39, Pellizer (1981) 35-49 and Gentili (1981) 18.

[11] On the application of the term "iambos" to poems not in iambic trimeter, cf. West (1974) 37-38.

[12] This point has been made by many scholars, but cf. West (1974) 31-32.

[13] See Rösler (1976) 301.

as obscene diction and picaresque narrative. The invective connotations of the term "iambos" in the fifth century are also strengthened by its connection with religious cult, notably the cults of Demeter and Dionysus.[14] Although the evidence for ritual abuse in festivals such as the Haloa, the Stenia and the Thesmophoria says nothing about iambic verse per se, the connection between iambs and ritual abuse is implicit in the name of Demeter's servant Iambe who, as recounted in the *Homeric Hymn to Demeter*, uses mockery to shock the goddess out of mourning for her lost daughter.[15] Thus Aristotle is able to use the verb ἰαμβίζειν at *Poet.* 1448b32 where he derives the name of the meter from the fact that it became associated with abuse (ὅτι ἐν τῷ μέτρῳ τούτῳ ἰάμβιζον ἀλλήλους).[16] When Aristotle says at *Poet.* 1449b7 that Crates "abandoned the iambic form" popular with the other Old Comic poets, he is referring to a movement away from personal abuse.[17] The iambos, in short, was for the Greeks the poetic mode of blaming, satire and ribaldry.[18]

---

[14] The most complete collection of sources for ritual invective can be found in Fluck (1931).

[15] Cf. Richardson (1971) 213ff.; Graf (1974) 224 s.v. γεφυρισμοί; Rusten (1977) 157-61.

[16] Aristotle states at *Poet.* 1449a10 that comedy arose out of the leaders of the phallic songs of cult (τὰ φαλλικά), implying a genealogical relationship between the invective of cult, the iambos, and comedy. While it is likely that the invective of the Ionian iambos and of Old Comedy does have its roots in cultic invective rituals, the evidence for this is controversial, and ultimately has little specific bearing on Old Comedy. Scholars tend either to trust Aristotle's testimony about τὰ φαλλικά and rely heavily on Semos of Delos' relatively late (2nd BC) account of phallic processions (as quoted by Athenaeus 622d = *FGH* 396F23), or to discount Aristotle and stress other equally problematic evidence. Herter (1947) and Giangrande (1963) fall into the first group. Pickard-Cambridge (1962) 132-159 argues for the theory of the *komos*, or begging procession as the origin of Old Comedy. As Henderson (1975) 17 sensibly states, while the cults surely provided the comic poets with a "general freedom to develop [their] method of attack as an art, ... the Ionian literary tradition of obscene and abusive iambic poetry seems a more direct artistic inspiration for the playwrights."

[17] τῶν δὲ Ἀθήνησιν Κράτης πρῶτος ἦρξεν ἀφέμενος τῆς ἰαμβικῆς ἰδέας καθόλου ποιεῖν λόγους καὶ μύθους [= Crates Test. 5KA]. Whether or not Aristotle's literary history here is correct is another matter. To say that Crates "abandoned the iambic form" seems rather categorical in view of the evidence we do have of his plays, which suggests that he did *not* abandon abuse entirely. Moreover, if Aristotle meant that because of Crates Old Comedy began to lose its resemblence to the iambos, this would neglect the strongly iambic nature of Aristophanes (who is later than Crates). Most likely, the emphasis is here on Crates' "construction of general plots," and we should take πρῶτος closely with ποιεῖν λόγους καὶ μύθους, understanding ἀφέμενος τῆς ἰαμβικῆς ἰδέας as referring to Crates' own particular stylistic tendencies, not to a chronological stage in the development of Old Comedy. See Else (1957) 203, and Bonanno (1972) 43.

[18] The same was true among the Romans; note Catullus' use of *iambus* to refer to his hendecasyllables (36. 5), and Horace *Carm.* 1.16.3, 24.

Although the iambos displayed a predilection for personal abuse, we must not forget that this abuse must also be considered as a function of generic convention. While this is hardly an eccentric statement, it bears emphasis here because of the frequently subjective ring of iambographic poetry. When an iambic poet engages in abuse he posits an animosity between the "I" of the poem and a target. Usually this "I" identifies himself as the poet, which encourages the audience to accept the incidents and characters of the poem as historical/autobiographical. A ψόγος, after all, takes the form of a direct provocation, a taunt or challenge that presumes a historical relationship with the target and implies a response from him. Since, however, as scholars have noted, iambic ψόγοι display certain conventions of diction, content and tone that are appropriate to that genre, while unacceptable in others,[19] it is reasonable to assume that generic considerations influenced the creation of a given iambic ψόγος just as much as, if not more than, personal rancor. We must be wary, in the end, of assuming that a ψόγος necessarily reflects a "real" hostility between the poet and his target, even in cases where the target may be a known historical figure.[20]

Although my methods in this study are primarily philological, I should note here that the more "anthropological" approaches to comedy and satire in relation to their social contexts also help to support my general argument. The cultic origin of the iambos and Old Comedy, to which I alluded above (n. 16), murky as it is in its detail, suggests in itself that socially prescribed obscenity existed in and for a setting in which cotidian norms and prohibitions were set aside.[21] The comparative

---

[19] Cf. West (1974) 25, Gentili (1981) 18, (1982) 14-27.

[20] On the relationship, for example, between Hipponax and the historical figure Bupalus, cf. L. Koenen (1977) 76 n. 14, and Rosen (1988). See also the remarks on Lycambes and Archilochus in Burnett (1983) 7.

[21] See Carrière (1979) 31, who, like many others who propose a "carnival" model for Old Comedy, draws on Bakhtin's (1968) discussion of the "Carnival" background to Rabelesian satire. Rösler (1986) discusses Bakhtin's theoretical construct in relation to Greek literature. Also see Meuli (1975). Halliwell (1984a) 16 takes an extreme view: "the techniques and practices of Aristophanic satire are based not on the premise of a didactic or edifying function for the poet's work, but on the conventions and presuppositions of a special festive freedom of speech, which is insulated from some of the normal requirements of social and political life in the city." J. Henderson was kind enough to show me a draft of an essay entitled "The Demos and the Comic Competition" (forthcoming in a volume to be published by Princeton University Press), in which he maintains that the "carnivalist" model, by separating the "real world" from the world of "mere entertainment," presents an incomplete picture of Old Comedy that offers no room for a poet's seriousness. Henderson is perhaps right to say that (technically speaking, anyway) "comic *festivals* [my emphasis] were not 'carnival' but civic business," but I would still regard the world of the comic *play itself*, as it unfolds upon the stage, as a world of "carnival." An atmosphere of "carnival," moreover, need not preclude all

research on the ritual background of "collective obscenity" in other cultures offers remarkable parallels to the same phenomenon in Greek society, and allows us to regard the social function of iambographic and comic obscenity as fundamentally similar.[22] To say that the iambos and Old Comedy fulfilled a similar "social function," of course, does not illuminate the specific ritual milieux in which the two genres arose. On that issue we are, unfortunately, still without adequate evidence. It does, however, allow us to posit a certain consciousness on the part of the poets active in these genres that the social context for which they were composing was in some sense "specialized" or "occasional." Even if (as is likely) the specific religious origins of the iambos and of comedy had receded in the minds of the audience and poet alike by the time we reach Archilochus on the one hand, and the institutionalization of comedy at the Dionysia in 486 on the other, the poets of both genres must have been aware that the audience for which they wrote expected and endorsed certain licenses of diction, gesture, costume, and authorial stance that would have been taboo, or at least abnormal, outside of the poetic occasion. It is important for us to keep this in mind, since the expectations of an audience and the poet's perception of his role in the community are formal considerations, existing prior to composition, which influenced the poet's manipulation of individual details.

The fifth century in Athens was an age of literary self-consciousness, sometimes, as we hear in the case of Euripides, even of bookishness. The poets of Old Comedy were no exception: it is readily apparent from the texts we have that they often freely referred to other comic poets, to tragedians, lyric poets and others. In many ways they offer the best evidence that there was a definite, if as yet unsystematic, sense of "literary history" in the fifth century. It should come as no surprise, therefore, as I argue in the ensuing chapters, that the comic poets came to realize, and subsequently exploited, the inherent affinity their poetry had with the iambos. While there were no doubt certain elements, especially at the level of diction, that the iambos and Old Comedy shared simply by virtue of their common goal of κωμῳδεῖν ὀνομαστί, my primary concerns in this study will be to affirm that the comic poets under-

---

seriousness of purpose in a work of literature. (Even Bakhtin [p. 12] emphasizes this, urging that we "stress the special philosophical and utopian character of festive laughter and its orientation towards the highest spheres.") The problem, of course, becomes how to interpret "seriousness" that occurs in such a context. As I attempt to show below in Chapter IV, the conventional (or read: "carnivalesque") elements of a comic play compel the audience to find seriousness beneath the surface details of the play.

[22] Reckford (1987) 443-467 provides a useful general account, with bibliography, of the comparative data relevant to Old Comedy.

stood the iambos as a strictly literary antecedent for their own work, to examine how certain distinctly iambographic features were incorporated into Old Comedy, and, finally, to suggest how my argument affects our understanding of the comic ψόγος not so much as an abstract social phenomenon, but rather as a literary construct.

CHAPTER II
IAMBOS AND OLD COMEDY

In this chapter we shall consider (1) the degree to which the comic poets of the fifth century were aware of the iambos as a discrete poetic genre, and (2) to what extent they perceived the generic relationship between their ψόγοι and iambographic ψόγοι, and, as a result, consciously adopted iambographic conventions. As these questions indicate, I shall be most concerned here to establish that the comic poet was aware of his debt to the iambic ψόγος. It will not be enough, therefore, simply to point out the various verbal connections between the two genres; in two overtly satirical types of poetry we will naturally find a certain amount of shared vocabulary. Henderson, for example, documents well the obscene vocabulary found in both the iambos and Old Comedy, but by itself this need not necessarily indicate conscious borrowing on the part of the comic poets.[1]

It is often said that the iambos was a moribund literary genre in the fifth century,[2] and while this judgment may be an exaggeration based on a lack of evidence, it seems generally valid. Still, even though it is impossible to point to any fifth-century iambic poet of distinction, it is surely significant that one of the few iambographers we do know of, Hermippus, was best known as a comic dramatist (first victory at the City Dionysia 435 BC). We may infer from the fact that Hermippus wrote iamboi as well as comic plays that there was at least some sort of audience for the non-dramatic iambos at this time.[3] Although we possess

---

[1] Though he does suggest as much (p. 17): cf. above, p. 4, n. 16.
[2] E.g., Cunningham (1971) 12: "After Hipponax the ἴαμβος is dead. The verse is taken over by Solon and Attic drama for other purposes, but disappeared with the society in which it alone flourished."
[3] Plato (*Legg.* 935e4) and Aristotle (*Pol.* 1336b20) refer to the performance of iamboi (in each case mentioned in conjunction with comic drama), although it is uncertain exactly what form these took. Athenaeus refers to Hermippus four times with the formula Ἕρμιππος ἐν (τοῖς) ἰάμβοις: 76c (= Hermippus fr. 2W), 461e (= 4W), 667d (= 7W), 700d (= 8W); cf. also Σ Aristoph. *Pl.* 701 (= 1W) and Σ *Av.* 1150 (= 3W). In 461e the phrase Ἕρμιππος ὁ κωμῳδοποιὸς ἐν τοῖς ἰάμβοις is followed by two lines in trochaic tetrameters, showing that by "iamboi" Athenaeus meant the poetic genre — the iambos — not the meter. Recognizing this, Meineke I.96 conjectured "Hermippum carminum probrosorum (ἰάμβων) volumen edidisse ... quorum alia trimetris iambicis, alia tetrametris trochaicis composita essent."

barely eight non-comic lines from Hermippus (frr. 3 and 5W are highly corrupt), even these display several points of contact with the Ionian iambos and Old Comedy. Athenaeus (461e) attests, for example that fr. 4W was intended as abuse, which affirms that the iambos was still felt to be a suitable genre for such an activity:

κυλικηγορήσων ἔρχομαι, οὐ τῶν Κυλικράνων εἷς ὑπάρχων, οὓς
χλευάζων Ἕρμιππος ... φησίν·
εἰς τὸ Κυλικράνων βαδίζων σπληνόπεδον ἀφικόμην·
εἶδον οὖν τὴν Ἡράκλειαν, καὶ μάλ' ὡραίαν πόλιν.

The humor of the passage, moreover, clearly lies in the pun on a proper name (Κυλικρᾶνες = "Cup-heads") and in the comic neologism σπληνόπεδον.[4] Both of these devices are prevalent in the iambos (especially in Hipponax) and Old Comedy.[5]

Fr. 5W (= Σ Aristoph. *Vesp.* 1169) shows obscenity in addition to neologism and punning:

ὕστερον δ' αὐτὴν †στρατηγὸν οὖς† ἀνειλωτημένην.
καὶ κασαλβάζουσαν εἶδον καὶ σεσαλακωνισμένην.

1 αὐτὴν Meineke: αὐτὸν καὶ Ald.   στρατηγῶν (στρατηγὸν Kaibel) οὖσαν εἰλωτισμένην Meineke   ἰλωπημένην Sitzler *J. f. cl. Ph.* 125 (1882) 159   2 σεσαλωκισμένην codd. corr. J. Schneider *Gr. dsch. Lex. s. v.*

(The text I print is a conflation of West's and Meineke's, V.1.3.[6])

---

[4] Some have suspected a corruption in this line. Schweighäuser reads σκληρόπεδον; *LSJ* suggests that the word is a false reading for σφηνόπεδον (= "wedge-shaped plain").

[5] Cf. Hipponax fr. 78.12Dg Λ[αυ]ριῶνα (a pun on the month Ταυρεών; on the form see Masson ad loc. 145 (who, however, reads Τ[αυριῶνα). The reading is uncertain, but if dung beetles (κάνθαροι) do appear at the end of the line, it is likely that a pun on λαύρη ("latrine"; cf. Hipponax fr. 95.10Dg) could stand in this context. For other puns on proper names in Hipponax, cf. fr. 177Dg: συκοτραγίδης (= Archil. 250W); probably Hipponax fr. 196.9Dg: Αἰσχυλίδης ("ft. patronymicum ironice fictum," Degani); fr. 127Dg: παρὰ Κυψοῦν (< Καλυψώ as a pun on κύπτω, *sensu obsceno*; cf. Archil. 42.2W: κύβδα in context of fellatio); Archil. fr. 168W: Ἐρασμονίδης Χαρίλαος; fr. 185W: Κηρυκίδης; fr. 331W: Πασιφίλη. Aristoph. *Nub.* 710: οἱ Κορίνθιοι = "bugs," *Equ.* 899: Κόπρειος. On Hipponax's fondness for neologism, cf. Degani's list of Hipponactean hapax formations (he lists 87, Degani [1983] xxviii), many of which clearly were coined for their comic potential, e.g. ποντοχάρυβδιν (126.1Dg), μεσσηγυδορποχέστης (171Dg).

[6] Meineke I. 99 is probably right to suggest that fr. 5 should be joined to fr. 4. The occurrence of εἶδον in both frr. makes for a smooth transition from one to the other, and suggests that the speaker may be reporting various sights he has seen. If the two are joined, then the feminine participles of fr. 5 must refer to the city of Heraclea mentioned in fr. 4, i.e. "I saw Heracleia — and a fine, young city she was! — but later (ὕστερον δ') I saw her ..." Athenaeus 461e makes clear that the Heracleia of fr. 4 refers to the Spartan foundation of that city in 426. Thucydides 3. 92-93 mentions that the city was

Κασαλβάζουσαν and σεσαλακωνισμένην are found elsewhere only in Aristophanes and both have obscene and/or abusive connotations there.⁷ The verb is formed from the noun κασαλβάς, meaning "whore" as in *Ecclesiazusae* 1106. Although the precise meaning of the verbal form, taking a direct object, is uncertain, the *Equites* passage makes it clear that it is used as an insult with a sexual coloring (perhaps "tease sexually"; cf. *LSJ* "abuse in a strumpet fashion," and Henderson [1975] 212). In this sense it is appropriate in the Hermippus fragment as a description of an anthropomorphized Heracleia, which, as Thucydides relates (see above n. 6) did not live up to the promises she had held out to her colonists.⁸ σεσαλακωνισμένην is a conflation of σαλάκων (= "pretentious person" as in Aristotle *Rhet.* 1391a2) and λακωνίζω (= "to ally with the Spartans"). Aristophanes himself conflates these two at *Vespae* 1169, punning on the political connotations of the -λακων- element. This background suggests to me the text I print, meaning: "but later [I saw] her [i.e. Heracleia] . . . 'turned into a helot' [cf. the *Suda* (1033 Adler) s.v. κατειλωτισμένος], sexually teasing and swaggering pretentiously."⁹

The only other attested iambographer likely to belong to the fifth century is the obscure poet named Diphilus (to be distinguished from the homonymous poet of New Comedy). One of the two scholiastic testimonia about him, Σ Pindar *Ol.* 10.83b (1.332.4Dr.) mentions that he composed iamboi.¹⁰ Meineke I.449 adduced Σ *Nubes* 96 (= Diphilus fr. 2 Bergk) as an indication that Diphilus can be dated prior to Aristophanes, and there seems little reason to doubt this:

πρῶτον μὲν γὰρ Δίφιλος εἰς Βοίδαν τὸν φιλόσοφον ὁλόκληρον συνέταξε ποίημα, δι' οὗ καὶ εἰς δουλείαν ἐρρυπαίνετο ὁ φιλό-

---

founded as an added defense against the Athenians, and describes how the whole endeavor failed because of the unduly harsh Spartan government.

⁷ Cf. *Equ.* 355: κασαλβάσω τοὺς ἐν Πύλῳ στρατηγούς.
⁸ See also Gomme (1962a) 399.
⁹ Cf. MacDowell (1971) 282 ad 1169. †στρατηγὸν οὒς† is still a mystery. It is possible that some of the corruption of the first verse lies in the order of the words. That is, if we place the notion of a "general" or "generals" at the end of the verse, putting punctuation after ἀνειλωτημένην, we might envisage some word or expression involving "general" as an object of κασαλβάζουσαν, as in *Equ.* 355 (cf. above, n. 7).
¹⁰ The scholiast confuses matters by referring to Diphilus as ὁ τὴν Θησηίδα ποιήσας, implying either that he wrote an epic "Theseid" as well as iamboi, or that his "Theseid" was iambic (or choliambic). West (1971) 61 denies, probably rightly, that a "serious" Theseid could have been composed in choliambs before the Alexandrian period.

σοφος· οὐ διὰ τοῦτο δὲ ἐχθρὸς ἦν· ἔπειτα Εὔπολις, εἰ καὶ δι' ὀλίγων ἐμνήσθη Σωκράτους, μᾶλλον ἢ Ἀριστοφάνης ἐν ὅλαις ταῖς Νεφέλαις αὐτοῦ καθήψατο.

The scholiast here wishes to show that when a poet ridicules someone, it does not necessarily mean that they were enemies. He mentions that Diphilus composed a "whole" (ὁλόκληρον) poem against a philosopher named Boidas (otherwise unknown), but that Boidas was not for this reason the poet's enemy (οὐ διὰ τοῦτο δὲ ἐχθρός ἦν). Although there is no specific indication here that Diphilus' poem was iambic, the very fact that it is alleged to be a poem of ridicule, which one could expect to evoke hostility from Boidas, in conjunction with our knowledge that he composed iamboi, leaves little doubt that this poem was in fact an iambos. The fact that this poem is mentioned in the same context as the abusive plays of Eupolis and Aristophanes suggests that the scholiast felt that Diphilus' personal invective was similar to that of a comic poet.

The evidence, limited as it is, is sufficient to show that there was some literary activity in the iambos even in the fifth century, and that the conventions of the fifth-century iambos were similar to those of the Ionian iambos. Hermippus' dual activity as an iambographer and a comic poet, moreover, signals an awareness that both genres were considered appropriate vehicles for the ψόγος.[11]

The status in the fifth century of the great representatives of the Ionian iambos, Archilochus and Hipponax, although not as well attested as we might expect,[12] confirms that they both were regarded as exemplars of the poetic ψόγος. Archilochus composed poetry in genres other than the iambos, notably elegy, and he was also honored with a cult on his native Paros.[13] This accounts for his ambivalent reputation throughout antiquity. Plato, for example, has Socrates class Archilochus alongside Homer and Hesiod at *Ion* 531a2,[14] and makes Adeimantus

---

[11] It is impossible to say whether Hermippus composed iamboi because he was influenced by the ἰαμβικὴ ἰδέα of the comedies he was composing, or whether he began composing comedies because he enjoyed the invective of his iamboi. As we shall see in the next chapter, the ἰαμβικὴ ἰδέα of comedy would have been a fairly recent innovation, for which Cratinus was largely responsible, and it is possible that Hermippus' iamboi were experiments influenced by the current trends in comedy.

[12] See von Blumenthal (1922) 2-3. For Hipponax cf. Jung (1929) 9-12.

[13] Nagy (1979) 304-5; Lefkowitz (1982) 31.

[14] This passage testifies to Archilochus' importance in the rhapsode's repertoire of the fifth-century. Earlier in the century Heraclitus implied as much when he said that Homer and Archilochus ought to be expelled from the (rhapsodic) competitions (DK 22 B42).

refer to him as σοφώτατος at *Resp.* 365c.¹⁵ But Archilochus was also regarded at this time as the abusive iambic poet *par excellence*. Pindar *Pyth.* 2.55 refers bluntly to Archilochus as ψογερός and sees his poetry as generically (and ideologically) opposed to his own poetry of praise (52-56):¹⁶

> ... ἐμὲ δὲ χρεών
> φεύγειν δάκος ἀδινὸν κακαγοριᾶν.
> εἶδον γὰρ ἑκὰς ἐὼν τὰ πόλλ' ἐν ἀμαχανίᾳ
> ψογερὸν Ἀρχίλοχον βαρυλόγοις ἔχθεσιν
> πιαινόμενον.

For Pindar, Archilochus' invective poetry amounts to the "bite of abusive speech"¹⁷ that will lead ultimately to a kind of poetic "resourcelessness" (ἀμαχανία).¹⁸

The fifth-century sophist Critias also disapproved of the Archilochian iambos. In DK 88 B44 (ap. Ael. *Var. Hist.* 10.13 = Tarditi Test. 46) he complains that Archilochus painted a degrading portrait of himself in his poems.¹⁹ At the climax of his tirade he states that Archilochus "spoke ill equally of friends and enemies" (ὅτι ὁμοίως τοὺς φίλους καὶ τοὺς ἐχθροὺς κακῶς ἔλεγε). This phrase, a perversion of the ethic of loving one's friends and hating one's enemies (cf. e.g., Plato *Resp.* 332d7), reflects Critias' understanding of the Archilochian ψόγος as indiscriminate abuse.

Archilochus' reputation in the fifth century is summed up well by Aristotle's quotation of Alcidamas (*Rhet.* 1398b11), who wondered how the Parians could honor as a σοφός a poet who wrote such "blasphemous" verse, i.e. a poet of invective: ... πάντες τοὺς σοφοὺς τιμῶσιν,

---

¹⁵ For favorable assessments of Archilochus, see also the following testimonia in Tarditi's collection: 74 (Heraclides Pont.); 23 (Ariston Chius ap. Philodem. *Poem.*); 34-38 (Cicero); 50, 53 (Dio Chrysostom).
¹⁶ Pindar was aware, however, that Archilochus was not exclusively a blame poet; cf. *Ol.* 9.1ff which alludes to an Archilochian hymn to Herakles, (= 324W); cf. also West (1974) 138, and Miller (1981) 140.
¹⁷ On δάκος here cf. Miller (1981) 137 n. 5.
¹⁸ Cf. Miller (1981) 140. Nagy (1979) 224, has shown how the vocabulary of this passage derives from the traditional terminology of blame poetry.
¹⁹ On this passage see Lefkowitz (1982) 27; also Rankin (1975) 324-34. Two ancient principles of literary criticism are at work here, first that one can extract biographical information from a person's poetry (Critias himself claims no other source than Archilochus' poetry: εἰ μὴ παρ' αὐτοῦ μαθόντες), and second that the character of one's poetry is a reflection of the character of the poet (as, e.g., in Agathon's portrait in Aristophanes' *Thesmo.*).

Πάριοι γοῦν Ἀρχίλοχον καίπερ βλάσφημον ὄντα τετιμήκασι. It was recognized at this period that Archilochus was a poet of immense stature, but his primary claim to fame seems to have remained his activity as a blame poet.[20]

Hipponax's reputation in the fifth century is even less well documented than that of Archilochus, but although it is probably true that he was less popular than Archilochus at this time,[21] his importance should not be underestimated. Hipponax, as far as we know, was never elevated, like Archilochus, to the level of Homer and Hesiod, nor did he become part of a rhapsode's repertoire. Archilochus had more diverse literary pretensions than Hipponax, who, by contrast, seems to have preferred rakish personae and picaresque narratives. But this is precisely what the comic poets seemed to love about Hipponax, as we shall see below.[22] Unlike Archilochus, Hipponax was uniformly thought of as an acerbic poet of the ψόγος.[23] Nearly all the *vitae* refer to his legendary quarrel with the sculptor Bupalus.[24] Pliny provides our earliest detailed account of the story (*NH* 36.11), recounting how Hipponax, in reaction to Bupalus' satirical sculpture of him, drove him to suicide with his vicious invective. Its similarity to the story of Archilochus and Lycambes is obvious, and it is likely that it arose by analogy.[25] Regardless of how the story developed, it clearly became emblematic of the particular sting of Hipponax's iambos.[26]

The two allusions to Hipponax in the fifth century, both in Aristophanes, confirm this reputation. At *Lysistrata* 360f the Old Men compare

---

[20] Gorgias is alleged to have called Plato a "new Archilochus" (νέον Ἀρχίλοχον) when Plato greeted him sarcastically with "ἥκει ἡμῖν ὁ καλός τε καὶ χρυσοῦς Γοργίας" (recounted by the hellenistic historian Hermippus (fr. 63 Wehrli = Athenaeus 505d). While the story is no doubt a fiction, the conceit of calling someone an incarnation of a famous person of old is found in the fifth century (cf. Cratinus 259KA [= Plutarch *Per.* 24.9], Aristophanes *Av.* 1009, Plato *Euthyph.* 11d), and we may assume that the expression "νέος Ἀρχίλοχος," referring to someone's abusive nature, was current at this time.

[21] Cf. Jung (1929) 9-11; Masson (1962) 33; Gerhard (1913) 1904-7 s. v. "Nachleben."

[22] For some of the more apparent connections between Hipponax and Old Comedy, cf. Henderson (1975) 19-22, Gerhard (1913) 1904 and Jung (1929) 10.

[23] Hipponax, like Archilochus, also composed in a variety of meters, but his fame rested almost exclusively on his choliambic poetry. Even his non-choliambic poetry can usually be considered "iambic."

[24] Cf. Degani (1983) 3-9 for the testimonia, to which we should add the passages from Aristophanes discussed below.

[25] First proposed by Welcker (1817) 14. See also Hendrickson (1925) 101-3. Pliny was the first to deny the truth of the Bupalus story on the grounds that one could find sculptures by Bupalus after the time of his alleged suicide. Cf. also Rosen (1988).

[26] Cf. Callimachus fr. 191. 1-4 (which mentions Βουπάλειον μάχην); also Horace *Epod.* 6.11-14.

the treatment they threaten to give to the Women to that suffered by
Bupalus at the hands of Hipponax:

εἰ νὴ Δί' ἤδη τὰς γνάθους τούτων τις ἢ δὶς ἢ τρὶς
ἔκοψεν ὥσπερ Βουπάλου, φωνὴν ἂν οὐκ ἂν εἶχον.

It has long been recognized, in fact, that this passage alludes specifically
to Hipponax frr. 121 and 122Dg:[27]

λάβετέ μεο ταἰμάτια, κόψω Βουπάλου[28] τὸν ὀφθαλμόν (fr. 121)

ἀμφιδέξιος γάρ εἰμι κοὐκ ἁμαρτάνω κόπτων (fr. 122)

This fragment may have begun a tetrameter poem, and as such the whole poem would be known as "the one in which Hipponax threatens to poke (κόπτειν) Bupalus in the eye." It seems, at any rate, that the verb κόπτειν is what sticks in Aristophanes' mind, as if this word of physical violence has special resonance in Hipponax's poetry.[29] In order for this allusion to have its full effect, we must assume that even the brief mention of Bupalus was sufficient to call to the minds of the audience not only the poetic quarrel he had with Hipponax but also the entire poetic tradition that this quarrel came to represent.

Aristophanes *Ranae* 659f mentions Hipponax by name in a context that associates the iambos with pain. In this scene Dionysus, having agreed to undergo torture at the hands of Aeacus in order to prove his claim to divinity, finds his tolerance of pain surprisingly human. When Xanthias rushes to point out that Dionysus in fact has felt pain, Dionysus tries to cover it up, alleging that he was merely remembering a verse from Hipponax:

ΔΙ: "Απολλον — ὅς που Δῆλον ἢ Πυθῶν' ἔχεις.
ΧΑ: ἤλγησεν· οὐκ ἤκουσας; ΔΙ: οὐκ ἔγωγ', ἐπεὶ
     ἴαμβον Ἱππώνακτος ἀνεμιμνησκόμην.[30]

---

[27] Jung (1929) 10, who connects this fragment with fr. 73.4-5W (= 132Dg, though Degani obelizes the entire line): ₍οἱ δέ μεο ὀδόντες ‖ ἐν ταῖς γ₍ινάθοισι πάντες <ἐκ>κεκινέαται; See also Masson (1962) 166, and below, p. 70, n. 29.

[28] West (= fr. 120) has Βουπάλῳ, implying that the genitive stems from the Aristophanic passage.

[29] Note also Hipponax fr. 8Dg: δοκέων ἐκεῖνον τῇ βακτηρίῃ κόψαι. Herodas alludes to this fragment in *Mim.* 8.60 (... τῇ βατηρίῃ κό[ψω), a programmatic poem in which his debt to Hipponax is openly acknowledged in v. 79.

[30] Σ *Ran.* 661 attributes the quotation to the obscure iambographer Ananius, which has led scholars to accuse Aristophanes of a mistake in attributing them to Hipponax. (Cf. Wilamowitz [1900] 65, and West [1972] 34). Apparently Ananius was such a close

Why does Dionysus claim to be thinking of Hipponax in the first place? Having just been struck by Aeacus, he cries out initially "Apollo!" and thinks quickly enough to complete the line with something applicable to that god. Yet in choosing a line from Hipponax he intends to explain away his painful outburst on the grounds that such a cry of pain would be appropriate when quoting from that poet. This implies, of course, that the audience would immediately associate the Hipponactean iambos with poetic contexts that involved personal attack, exclamations of pain and the like.

So far we have seen that the iambos was properly perceived in the fifth century as a genre of abuse and satire, and that Archilochus and Hipponax were considered its paradigmatic representatives. But before we can argue that the iambos had a formative influence on Old Comedy we must establish first that the comic poets were conscious that their poetic activity was generically similar. The evidence from Hermippus and Diphilus has given us some indication that the iambos was in fact felt to be related to Old Comedy, and we shall presently find corroboration of this in two other kinds of evidence: 1) quotations of or allusion to iambographers in the comic poets chosen specifically because they were felt to be appropriate to a kindred genre, and 2) passages from comedy which address its relationship with the iambos.

It is, of course, a delicate matter to evaluate the particular significance of a literary allusion or quotation. Some examples of iambographic diction in comic drama make a *prima facie* case for some sort of relationship between the two genres, but do not establish a specific mechanism of influence.[31] Comic poets, moreover, alluded to many non-iam-

---

imitator of Hipponax' style that commentators in antiquity had difficulty distinguishing the two (cf. Heraclides Pont. [ap. Athen. 625c]: οὗ μνημονεύει Ἀνάνιος ἢ Ἱππῶναξ ἐν τοῖς ἰάμβοις οὕτως . . .; and Hephaestion 5 who mentions a dispute over whether Hipponax or Ananius discovered the choliambic meter). Ten Brink (1851) 78, went so far as to suggest that "Ananius" was a pseudonym used by Hipponax in order to attack his enemies more easily. If the line really was by Ananius, it remains possible that Aristophanes had Dionysus *deliberately* confuse him with Hipponax as a joke. Such a joke, of course, would presume, as Masson (1962) 33 points out, widespread familiarity with these poets.

[31] Hipponax fr. 37Dg is a case in point:
οὐκ ἀτταγᾶς τε καὶ λαγοὺς καταβρύκων,
οὐ τηγανίτας σησάμοισι φαρμάσσων
οὐδ' ἀτταινίτας κηρίοισιν ἐμβάπτων.

This fragment displays asyndeton, homoioteleuton, an exaggerated obsession with food and an overall verbal balance of clauses typical of many passages in comedy (e.g., the exchange between the Sausage-seller and the Paphlagonian [see below p. 69] at *Equ.* 284-97; or *Ach.* 595-97:
ὅστις· πολίτης χρηστός, οὐ σπουδαρχίδης,

bographic poets, and more often than not such passages seem not to have any bearing on the development of the comic genre.[32] I shall examine, therefore, only those passages which have intrinsic relevance for the connection between the two genres, and I shall not be concerned to compile an exhaustive list of all the times a word, phrase, motif or poetic conceit in comedy can be paralleled in the iambos.

I. Of the five passages in which Aristophanes quotes Archilochus verbatim[33] one seems to show him using the quotation for an invective purpose similar to that of the original *sedes*.

Aristophanes *Acharnenses* 118-20 (cf. Archilochus fr. 187W):

ἐγᾦδ' ὅς ἐστι, Κλεισθένης ὁ Σιβυρτίου.
ὦ θερμόβουλον πρωκτὸν ἐξυρημένε.
τοιόνδε δ', ὦ πίθηκε, τὸν πώγων' ἔχων ...

The scholia to this passage remark that Aristophanes here "parodies"[34] the Archilochian line (187W): τοιήνδε δ' ὦ πίθηκε τὴν πυγὴν ἔχων.[35] It is likely that the Archilochian fragment came from the epode containing the ainos of the fox and the monkey, in which the fox ridicules the monkey's bare buttocks (the monkey leans over, caught in a trap).[36] Fr. 185.1-2W shows that this ainos was probably an invective vehicle against human targets: ἐρέω τιν' ὕμιν αἶνον, ὦ Κηρυκίδη, ἀχνυμένῃ σκυτάλῃ

ἀλλ' ἐξ ὅτου περ ὁ πόλεμος, στρατωνίδης,
σὺ δ' ἐξ ὅτου περ πόλεμος, μισθαρχίδης.
Cf. also Archil. fr. 115W and compare Comoed. fr. adesp. 1325K, on which see below, p. 47). Yet there is nothing here to indicate that such elements, when they occur in comedy, were taken over directly from the iambos. On the diction of this fragment, see further Degani (1973) 103-4 and (1975) 113-120.

[32] Cf. Aristophanic quotations from or allusions to Homer (e.g., *Equ.* 197-201, *Pax* 1089-94, *Ran.* 1034) or the lyric poets (cf. especially *Av.* 904-59). The references to tragedy are, of course, more complicated, since paratragedy, at least in the fifth century, seems to have become *de rigueur* in comedy (no doubt because the two types of drama were performed on the same occasion) and as such one may say that paratragic passages intrinsically reflect an aspect of comedy's development. But such passages never seem to call attention to a generic debt to tragedy.

[33] *Ach.* 120; *Pax* 1298; *Av.* 869; *Lys.* 1257; *Ran.* 704. See Hauvette (1905) 90-96.

[34] Here with the sense of "adapt, imitate, borrow, or paraphrase" as well as "ridicule, burlesque." See Householder (1944) 1-9, and Degani (1982) 12-33.

[35] The line (according to Σ R 119) is apparently also a parody of Euripides' ὦ θερμόβουλον σπλάγχνον (= fr. 858 Nauck), and it seems as if Aristophanes combines an allusion to the iambographer and the tragedian.

[36] On this ainos, see West (1971) 71 and 72 ad frr. 185-87.

(i.e. "an ainos bearing a sorrowful message"),[37] and we may assume that the πίθηκος of fr. 187W represents one of these targets. Aristophanes adapts the Archilochian line to ridicule the notorious effeminacy of Cleisthenes, substituting πώγων' for the original πυγήν (sarcastically, of course; the audience would know how inappropriate the beard would be on Cleisthenes). The preceding verse (119) in Aristophanes, however, works in a reference to this πυγήν with the phrase πρωκτὸν ἐξυρημένε. That is, the fox in the fable ridicules the natural nakedness of the monkey's buttocks, which are prominently exposed because he is bent over. The speaker of 119 (Dicaeopolis) suggests that even Cleisthenes' buttocks have been shaven, and a connection to the monkey of 120 is apparent only if the audience has the entire Archilochian ψόγος in mind. Aristophanes has understood that the fable is used by Archilochus to attack an individual, and by incorporating it into his own attack on Cleisthenes acknowledges that he and Archilochus are engaged in a similar poetic endeavor.

Two other Aristophanic quotations from Archilochus indicate a point of connection between the iambos and Old Comedy other than invective. This is in the realization that both genres, insofar as they engaged in individual and social criticism, had a fundamentally didactic pretence. Even though the attacks of an iambic or comic poet against a given target often appear to be personally motivated, behind them lies most often the pretence of alerting the audience to the moral danger of harboring such individuals. Aristophanes himself offers perhaps the classic statement of this in the parabasis of *Vespae* (1029-37):[38]

οὐδ' ὅτε πρῶτόν γ' ἦρξε διδάσκειν, ἀνθρώποις φήσ' ἐπιθέσθαι,
ἀλλ' Ἡρακλέους ὀργήν τιν' ἔχων τοῖσι μεγίστοις ἐπιχειρεῖν,
θρασέως ξυστὰς εὐθὺς ἀπ' ἀρχῆς αὐτῷ τῷ καρχαρόδοντι,
οὗ δεινόταται μὲν ἀπ' ὀφθαλμῶν Κύννης ἀκτῖνες ἔλαμπον,

---

[37] On ἀχνυμένῃ σκυτάλῃ, see West (1971) 72; also now S. West (1988), who prefers the nominative to the dative, p. 47.

[38] In later antiquity, Old Comedy was seen by its sympathetic critics primarily as a didactic genre concerned with ridiculing bad politicians and improving the souls of the audience. Cf., for example, Dio Chrysostom *Orat. Tars.* 33.9-11, who likens the activity of τὸ ψέγειν to that of a good philosopher (and as such claims that Archilochus was more like a philosopher than a comic poet, who mitigated his acerbity with "flattery" and jokes). Dio in fact supposes that Archilochus chose blame poetry because he saw that men had a greater need of moral correction than of praise! Cf. also Horace *Sat.* 1.4.3 on the didactic impulse of the poets of Old Comedy; also Platonius (Koster I.6-8) . . . ἄδειαν οἱ τὰς κωμῳδίας συγγράφοντες εἶχον τοῦ σκώπτειν καὶ στρατηγοὺς καὶ δικαστὰς τοὺς κακῶς δικάζοντας καὶ τῶν πολιτῶν τινας ἢ φιλαργύρους ἢ συζῶντας ἀσελγείᾳ.

ἑκατὸν δὲ κύκλῳ κεφαλαὶ κολάκων οἰμωξομένων ἐλιχμῶντο
περὶ τὴν κεφαλήν, φωνὴν δ' εἶχεν χαράδρας ὄλεθρον τετοκυίας,
φώκης δ' ὀσμήν, Λαμίας δ' ὄρχεις ἀπλύτους, πρωκτὸν δὲ καμήλου.
τοιοῦτον ἰδὼν τέρας οὔ φησιν δείσας καταδωροδοκῆσαι,
ἀλλ' ὑπὲρ ὑμῶν ἔτι καὶ νυνὶ πολεμεῖ·

In this passage the poet combines the claim that his ridicule serves moral purposes (ἐπιθέσθαι... τοῖσι μεγίστοις [sc. who were most corrupt]; ὑπὲρ ὑμῶν... πολεμεῖ) with a comical digression on Cleon that displays several elements found also in the iambos. In particular we may compare the diction involving testicles, the anus and foul smells in 1035 to Henderson's list, (1975) 19-24, of sexual and scatological obscenities in the iambos, and in particular we may note the following: ὄρχις (Hipp. 95.3Dg), πρωκτός (Hipp. 107.32Dg), πυγή (Archil. 187W; Hipp. 92.2Dg, 92.15Dg); σάθη (Archil. 25.2, 43.1, 82.4W); τράμις (Archil. 283W; Hipp. 133Dg); φάλης (Hipp. 34, 95.3Dg [?]). Also, the punning obscene name, as in Κύννα (1032), is a device common in the iambos.[39] But even more significant is the stance of the poet: boastful, self-righteous and socially-minded. Here, Cleon comes under attack as the corrupt politician, and Aristophanes' invective is portrayed as a social service rather than as a private feud.[40] Archilochus too tries to use public humiliation against his target Lycambes in fr. 172W, proclaiming that he will make him a laughingstock of the community (vv. 3-4): νῦν δὲ δὴ πολὺς ‖ ἀστοῖσι φαίνεαι γέλως.[41]

The didactic pretence of the iambos and comedy, however, was not limited to attacks on individuals, and the satirical bent of both genres often led the poets to outright social criticism. At Pax 603f Aristophanes quotes a phrase from Archilochus that was clearly used originally in a context of political exhortation:

EP: ὦ λιπερνῆτες γεωργοί, τἀμὰ δὴ ξυνίετε
ῥήματ', εἰ βούλεσθ' ἀκοῦσαι τήνδ' ὅπως ἀπώλετο.[42]

---

[39] On this name cf. MacDowell (1971) 266.
[40] For another programmatic statement in Aristophanes about teaching the public through comedy cf. Ach. 655-64.
[41] Note also the "Cologne Archilochus" (P. Col. II.58 = fr. 196aW) vv. 22-23, where the speaker states his desire to avoid public humiliation: [ὅ]πως ἐγὼ γυναῖκα τ[ο]ιαύτην ἔχων ‖ [γεί]τοσι χάρμ' ἔσομαι.
[42] I read λιπερνῆτες for σοφώτατοι along with Platnauer (1964), who follows Dindorf, even though Σ R does seem to have read the latter. Cf. Platnauer ad loc. p. 120 for a sound explanation of the emendation. The context in Aristophanes is especially appropriate for λιπερνῆτες over σοφώτατοι: the chorus has just asked Hermes why the gods have neglected men for so long. Hermes responds with some impatience because

From the scholiast we learn that Aristophanes (as well as Cratinus = fr. 211KA) was paraphrasing Archilochus (= fr. 109W):

<ὦ> λιπερνῆτες πολῖται, τἀμὰ δὴ συνίετε
ῥήματα.

λιπερνῆτες is a word of uncertain origin and meaning, but clearly used as a term of abuse. We cannot find agreement among the various ancient explanations: Photius suggests λιποπόλεις ἢ πένητες, Hesychius ὁ ἐκ πλουσίου πένης, ἢ ἐξ ἀγροῦ εἰς πόλιν πεφευγώς, ἢ ὁ λιπόπολις. Nevertheless, the line seems to have been well known in the fifth century; in addition to its appearance in Aristophanes and Cratinus, Eupolis also alludes to it (though without the λιπερνῆτες) in fr. 392.1-2KA:

ἀλλ' ἀκούετ' ὦ θεαταὶ τἀμὰ καὶ ξυνίετε
ῥήματ'.

The apparent celebrity of the Archilochian line among the comic poets does seem to indicate an awareness that their abusive social criticism also had antecedents in the Ionian iambographers.[43]

In the parabasis of *Ranae*, Aristophanes, in the process of giving political advice, again quotes Archilochus:

εἰ δὲ ταῦτ' ὀγκωσόμεσθα κἀποσεμνυνούμεθα,
τὴν πόλιν καὶ ταῦτ' ἔχοντες κυμάτων ἐν ἀγκάλαις,
ὑστέρῳ χρόνῳ ποτ' αὖθις εὖ φρονεῖν οὐ δόξομεν. (703-5)

The scholiast on this line (= Archilochus fr. 213W) says that v. 704 comes from the Archilochian line ψυχὰς ἔχοντες κυμάτων ἐν ἀγκάλαις.[44] While it is impossible to place this line in a larger context, it does seem likely that it comes from a poem of political exhortation.[45] If this is

---

the answer ought to be obvious — Pheidias!

[43] Cf. also Archilochus fr. 91W, a relatively long papyrus fragment which seems to have been an extended poem of a political nature. Plutarch (*Praec. ger. reip.* 6) preserves two lines that fit in well at vv. 14-15 of the papyrus, and suggest that the poem concerned some threat to the island of Thasos (cf. Lasserre [1958] 42). The fragment mentions at v. 2 people who are ν]ήπιοι φρένα, which seems to indicate that the poet was taking to task some group of citizens.

[44] The scholiast rejects Didymus' attribution to Aeschylus.

[45] Lasserre (1958) 75-78 (frr. 279-93) places this fr. (his fr. 282) in a group of lines which, he suggests, may come from a poem fantasizing about the Isle of the Blessed (in the context of urging the Thasians to emigrate to another country). This is, fundamentally, pure speculation, but he is probably right that the general nature of the poem is

so, then its appearance in the parabasis of *Ranae* is all the more appropriate since Aristophanes is there giving political advice,[46] and it demonstrates again Aristophanes' awareness that the didactic stance of the iambographer was appropriate for the comic poet.[47]

Even Hipponax, whose poems rarely seem to address concerns beyond the strictly personal, conspicuously treats his target Bupalus on several occasions as a social scourge. I refer to the fragments in which the poet speaks metaphorically of his ἐχθρός as φαρμακός, i.e. as ritual scapegoat chosen by the citizens to purify the city. Tzetzes (*Chil.* 5.728ff.) preserves in his narrative "τί τὸ κάθαρμα" several Hipponactean fragments that mention the φαρμακός (= frr. 26-30Dg). It is uncertain whether these come from one poem (Tzetzes gives us no indication), nor can we affirm that they were all directed against Bupalus.[48] The φαρμακός-motif also occurs at frr. 107.49, 126.3-4 and possibly 203Dg. Its recurrence seems to indicate that Hipponax was particularly fond of it:

---

political.
[46] Political satire and exhortation are, of course, important elements of the comic parabases. Sifakis (1971) 61 suggests that the parabasis was a 5th C. innovation, arguing both from the fact that the comic poets themselves saw it as a recent invention (e.g. *Equ.* 507-9) and that the themes of the eppirhematic syzygies delivered by the chorus — often abusive and satirical — would not be suitable for a *poet* to deliver publicly until the free atmosphere of the maturing Athenian democracy. If so, one must ask whether there was any specific correlation between the development of the parabases and the iambic elements of the comedy. One is tempted, for example, to see in the peculiarly abusive and didactic parabases a comic poet acting in a role akin to that of the earlier iambographer. But satire, abuse and obscenity are hardly limited to the parabases, and it would be nearly impossible to argue that the parabasis as a literary construct came into existence in order to emulate the subjective stance of the iambographers. Whatever the exact origins of the parabasis as we find it in Aristophanes, it does seem that the particular admonitory/abusive/didactic nature arose as a function of fifth-century *parrhesia* and its tolerance of abusive humor.
[47] It may also be significant that a highly invective and humorous (ant)ode (706-17) immediately follows the quotation from Archilochus, attacking a relatively insignificant citizen, the bathkeeper Cleigenes. (Probably, however, he was a demagogue of some sort as well; cf. L. Radermacher, [1954] 244 for the meager prosopographical evidence about him; At v. 715 he is referred to as οὐκ εἰρηνικός, implying that he was mentioned because of his politics as well as his profession; cf. Stanford [1963] 133). While the ode is clearly meant to raise a smile, there is an underlying pretense of seriousness that allies it with the preceding epirrhema and the subsequent antepirrhema. The syzygy, therefore, represents two facets of social satire, both of which are found in the Ionian iambos. The quotation from Archilochus evokes the self-righteous stance of the protreptic poet, the abusive antode demonstrates the biting and witty diction that such a poet has at his service.
[48] Cf. Masson (1962) 109, who suggests that fr. 29Dg may be directed against several targets (perhaps Bupalus and Arete, as Degani suggests ad fr. 29, p. 44).

Fr. 26Dg: πόλιν καθαίρειν καὶ κράδῃσι βάλλεσθαι
Fr. 27Dg: δεῖ δ' αὐτὸν ἐς φαρμακὸν †ἐκποιήσασθαι†
Fr. 28Dg: κἀφῇ παρέξειν ἰσχάδας τε καὶ μᾶζαν
            καὶ τυρόν, οἷον ἐσθίουσι φαρμακοί
Fr. 29Dg: πάλαι γὰρ αὐτοὺς προσδέκονται χάσκοντες
            κράδας ἔχοντες ὡς ἔχουσι φαρμακοῖς
Fr. 30Dg: λιμῷ γένηται ξηρός· ἐν δὲ τῷ θύμῳ
            φαρμακὸς ἀχθεὶς ἑπτάκις ῥαπισθείη.
Fr. 126Dg: Μοῦσά μοι Εὐρυμεδοντιάδεω τὴν ποντοχάρυβδιν,
            τὴν ἐγγαστριμάχαιραν, ὃς ἐσθίει οὐ κατὰ κόσμον,
            ἔννεφ', ὅπως ψηφῖδι <κακῇ> κακὸν οἶτον ὄληται
            βουλῇ δημοσίῃ παρὰ θῖν' ἁλὸς ἀτρυγέτοιο.[49]

Although φαρμακός is first attested in Hipponax, it was by his time already an ancient term for a public scapegoat, an individual selected for public beating and exile.[50] To call someone a φαρμακός, then, means that that person's offence has taken on public dimensions, that the individual is a public menace as well as a private enemy. Whether or not Hipponax' quarrels were in fact worthy of assuming such social importance is irrelevant; what matters is that he views himself in these contexts as a spokesman for the people. By comparing his enemies to φαρμακοί, the poet holds them responsible (no doubt in jest) for the city's ills, as well as for his own private grievances. As we have seen above, this attitude, public service through personal abuse, underlies much of the invective of Old Comedy.

It should not surprise us, therefore, to find the φαρμακός-motif in Old Comedy as well. In Aristophanes it occurs three times as follows:

---

[49] Fr. 126Dg, although obviously from a poem quite distinct from the others (it is in dactylic hexameters and is clearly a homeric parody) indicates that the target is being treated as a φαρμακός (public stoning by the sea). This has led scholars to suggest that the "son of Eurymedon" here is a cipher for Bupalus. See Koenen (1959) 112-115 for other possible reasons for a connection with Bupalus.

[50] See Masson (1962) 113 for bibliography on the word and its semantics. On the scapegoat ritual in Greek religion, see Bremmer (1983) 299-320, with further bibliography, n. 2.

1) *Equites* 1402-05:
εὖ γ' ἐπενόησας οὗπέρ ἐστιν ἄξιος,
πόρναισι καὶ βαλανεῦσι διακεκραγέναι.
καί σ' ἀντὶ τούτων εἰς τὸ πρυτανεῖον καλῶ
εἰς τὴν ἕδραν θ', ἵν' ἐκεῖνος ἦσθ' ὁ φαρμακός.

2) *Ranae* 730-33:
... τοῖς δὲ χαλκοῖς καὶ ξένοις καὶ πυρρίαις
καὶ πονηροῖς κἀκ πονηρῶν εἰς ἅπαντα χρώμεθα
ὑστάτοις ἀφιγμένοισιν, οἷσιν ἡ πόλις πρὸ τοῦ
οὐδὲ φαρμακοῖσιν εἰκῇ ῥᾳδίως ἐχρήσατ' ἄν.

3) Fr. 655KA:
πόθεν δ' ἐγώ σοι συγγενής, ὦ φαρμακέ;

In the passage from *Equites*, Demos closes the play by speaking of Cleon and his worthlessness. Cleon is here referred to as a φαρμακός, and since the entire play is, in one sense, a sustained attack on him from a stance of political and moral self-righteousness, the appellation is most appropriate. He is the one whose exile from politics will benefit the city.

In the second passage, from *Ranae*, the Coryphaeus says hyperbolically that the city has been trusting men more vile than those who would be used as ritual scapegoats in former times. Although he does not single out any individual as a φαρμακός, he does imply that the most morally corrupt and despicable citizens (πονηροί) would play the role well.

Fr. 655KA may use the word as a general epithet of abuse, meaning a "rascal" or "rogue," but it seems difficult to ignore its specific implications, and probably conveys the nuance "your character and behavior make you a public nuisance and a threat to civility."[51]

We have in addition a fragment from Eupolis' *Demoi* (fr. 132KA) which is remarkably reminiscent of Hipponax' φαρμακός fragments:

ὃν χρῆν ἔν <τε> ταῖς τριόδοις κἀν τοῖς ὀξυθυμίοις
προστρόπαιον τῆς πόλεως κάεσθαι τετριγότα

Kock (ad loc. p. 290) suggests that the fragment comes from the parabasis of the play, in which the poet speaks of a depraved politician "qui multo acerbiorem poenam meruerit quam comicorum cavillationem."

---

[51] Note also the vocative at *Plut.* 454: ὦ κάθαρμα.

The object of the speaker's enmity is considered a pollution to the city (προστρόπαιον τῆς πόλεως), who ought to be sacrificed by burning.[52]

It remains impossible, of course, to say whether these comic passages were directly inspired by Hipponax' use of the φαρμακός-motif. It does not, however, seem unlikely, in view of the fact that the comic poets' professed role as public teacher and moral corrector, as we have seen, was felt to be similar to that of the iambographer.[53]

II. Nowhere in extant comedy does a poet ever have occasion to make an explicit connection between the iambos and comic drama. Nevertheless, there are two passages in Aristophanes that indicate how conscious he was of his iambographic heritage. The first occurs in the great parodos of *Ranae*:

>   βούλεσθε δῆτα κοινῇ
>   σκώψωμεν Ἀρχέδημον,
>   ὃς ἑπτέτης ὢν οὐκ ἔφυσε φράτερας;
>
>   νυνὶ δὲ δημαγωγεῖ
> 420 ἐν τοῖς ἄνω νεκροῖσι,
>   κἄστιν τὰ πρῶτα τῆς ἐκεῖ μοχθηρίας.

---

[52] Cf. Tzetzes *Chil.* 5.737ff. :
τέλος πυρὶ κατέκαιον ἐν ξύλοις τοῖς ἀγρίοις,
καὶ τὴν σποδὸν εἰς θάλασσαν ἔρραινον εἰς ἀνέμους
εἰς καθαρμὸν τῆς πόλεως . . . νοσούσης;

[53] The fact that Callimachus (fr. 90Pf.) preserves in a hexameter from the *Aetia* Hipponax' peculiar scansion of φαρμακός (long second alpha) may provide some evidence for the direct influence of Hipponax' use of the word on later writers: ἔνθ' Ἄβδηρ' οὗ νῦν .[. . .]λεω φαρμακὸν ἀγινεῖ. (Cf. Masson [p. 113] on the mostly unsatisfactory attempts to explain the lengthened alpha in linguistic terms.) Hipponax and Callimachus are the only authors we know of to scan φαρμακός in this way, and the word is well attested (with short alpha) in the intervening period. It seems probable, therefore, that Callimachus was alluding to Hipponax' use of the word. The context does not tell us anything that would connect it explicitly with Hipponax: the *Diegesis* says that the poem was an aition of the φαρμακός ritual in Abdera (cf. Ovid *Ibis* 467 and Σ ad loc. Call. fr. 90 *Dieg.* II), and as such the word no doubt refers to an actual ritual scapegoat rather than to the metaphorical scapegoat in Hipponax. If Callimachus was alluding to Hipponax, we cannot say why he did (perhaps simply a display of erudition), but it may be significant that Abdera was originally an *Ionian* city, having been founded in the 7th C. by Clazomenae, where Hipponax is said to have gone into exile; cf. Degani (1983) Testim. 7 (Suda), 9a (Σ Hor. *Epod.* 6.14), 25 (Sulpicia, *Sat.* v. 6), and note fr. 17, beginning ὦ Κλαζομένιοι — a detail which strengthens the connection between Hipponax and Callimachus. Such a connection could reflect the notoriety of Hipponax' φαρμακός-poem(s) in antiquity.

> τὸν Κλεισθένους δ' ἀκούω
> ἐν ταῖς ταφαῖσι πρωκτὸν
> τίλλειν ἑαυτοῦ καὶ σπαράττειν τὰς γνάθους.
>
> 425 κἀκόπτετ' ἐγκεκυφώς,
> κἄκλαε κἀκεκράγει
> Σεβῖνον ὅστις ἐστὶν Ἀναφλύστιος.
>
> καὶ Καλλίαν γέ φασι
> τοῦτον τὸν Ἱπποβίνου[54]
> κύσθου λεοντῆν ναυμαχεῖν ἐνημμένον.

This song marks the entrance of the chorus of mystic initiates, and although the specific religious occasion is difficult to determine,[55] there is little doubt that the lines quoted above have affinities with the ritualized invective that accompanied the Eleusinian Gephyrismos.[56] The song is self-conscious invective. Earlier, in the first strophe of the ode (372-76) the chorus sings of their intention to engage in playful abuse (χώρει νυν πᾶς ‖ ... ἐγκρούων ‖ κἀπισκώπτων ‖ καὶ παίζων καὶ χλευάζων). In 416-17 (βούλεσθε δῆτα κοινῇ ‖ σκώψωμεν Ἀρχέδημον) the chorus deliberately calls attention to the activity of abuse itself, and to the communal nature (κοινῇ) of this activity. There follows a ψόγος against several citizens, which contains several points of diction reminiscent of the iambos. Hipponax 133Dg: †ἔξ† τίλλοι τις αὐτοῦ τὴν τράμιν †ὑποργάσαι evidently describes the same activity as the obscene phrase

---

[54] With Ἱπποβίνου I retain the reading of the MSS. Coulon prints Sternbach's Ἱπποκίνου.

[55] The literature on the controversy is immense, and finds scholars divided basically into two camps: those who believe that it represents a synthesis of various religious rituals, and those who try to associate it with a specific festival. The main problem is that there are very clear Eleusinian elements depicted, but the lyrics seem to emphasize Iacchus to a degree uncharacteristic of the Eleusinian procession. See Radermacher (1954) 184, and Segal (1961) 222, who concludes that "Aristophanes has combined a number of already related cult practices, a procedure facilitated by the fusion between the different aspects of Dionysus in the latter half of the fifth century." Most recently, however, Graf (1974) 40-50, has argued that all the various religious elements depicted in the parodos (e.g., the λείμων of the underworld, the Gephyrismos ritual, the μεμυημένοι and the Iacchus song) can be related to the mysteries at Eleusis. Segal 236 n. 44 offers a concise summary of the most important approaches to the problem; cf. Graf 40-50 for bibliography.

[56] Cf. Fluck (1931) 52ff. ; Graf (1974) 45-46; Rusten (1977) 157-61. Note also the iambic meter of this section.

"plucking the anus" (πρωκτὸν τίλλειν, 423-24); cf. also Hipponax 107.32Dg: ν]ενυχμένωι πρωκτῶ[ι, where the participle is probably from νύσσω = "pierce"). κύσθου in 430 also represents a class of obscene words first encountered in iambographic diction.[57] The three puns on proper names (here obscene too), Σεβῖνον (< βινέω); Ἀναφλύστιος (< ἀναφλάω = δέφομαι "masturbate"); τὸν Ἱπποβίνου (= "son of Horse-fucker") have a similar background (note also 439, Κόρινθος = "Corinthian/ bedbug"). Archilochus has Πασιφίλη (331W, which I accept as genuine, *pace* West), Λεώφιλος (115W), Ἐρασμονίδης Χαρίλαος (168W), Κηρυκίδης (185W),[58] while Hipponax offers Αἰσχυλίδης (196.9Dg), Πανδώρη (107.48Dg), Σάννος (129a.1, = "Penis"; see Degani ad loc. p. 132), Φλυήσιος (51.2Dg, used of Hermes < φλάω). Such iambic diction, combined with the fact that the chorus is reenacting a religious procession that was known to involve abusive αἰσχρολογία, suggests that Aristophanes had in mind the connection between the literary iambos and its ritual origins. But is there any evidence that he saw a relationship between this iambic background and Old Comedy? The quasi-parabatic anapaests of the chorus (354-71) that precede the above ψόγος of 420-34 suggest that he did:

εὐφημεῖν χρὴ κἀξίστασθαι τοῖς ἡμετέροισι χοροῖσιν,
355 ὅστις ἄπειρος τοιῶνδε λόγων ἢ γνώμην μὴ καθαρεύει,
ἢ γενναίων ὄργια Μουσῶν μήτ᾽ εἶδεν μήτ᾽ ἐχόρευσεν,
μηδὲ Κρατίνου τοῦ ταυροφάγου γλώττης Βακχεῖ᾽ ἐτελέσθη,
ἢ βωμολόχοις ἔπεσιν χαίρει μὴ 'ν καιρῷ τοῦτο ποιοῦσιν,
ἢ στάσιν ἐχθρὰν μὴ καταλύει μηδ᾽ εὔκολός ἐστι πολίταις,
360 ἀλλ᾽ ἀνεγείρει καὶ ῥιπίζει κερδῶν ἰδίων ἐπιθυμῶν,
ἢ τῆς πόλεως χειμαζομένης ἄρχων καταδωροδοκεῖται,
ἢ προδίδωσιν φρούριον ἢ ναῦς, ἢ τἀπόρρητ᾽ ἀποπέμπει
ἐξ Αἰγίνης Θωρυκίων ὢν εἰκοστολόγος κακοδαίμων,
ἀσκώματα καὶ λίνα καὶ πίτταν διαπέμπων εἰς Ἐπίδαυρον,

---

[57] Henderson (1975) 19-24. Note also 409-13, where the prurient chorus describes how it caught a glimpse of a girl's breast as she leaned over. While this is not κωμῳδεῖν ὀνομαστί, before Old Comedy the obscenity was at home only in the iambos. On κύπτω in the iambos in an obscene sense see Henderson 22 and cf. Hipponax frr. 24 and 127Dg (with Degani ad loc. p. 131), and Archilochus 42W. Note that the son of Cleisthenes is described above by the chorus as ἐγκεκυφώς, as he violently bemoans his lost lover.

[58] See Bonanno (1980) 65-88. Whether these names represent historical or fictional figures is less relevant than whether or not the poet puns on them. It is mistaken to think that in order for a proper name to be "significant," it *must* be fictional. I have argued elsewhere (1988), for example, that Hipponax puns on the name of the historical Bupalus (= Bou-phallos).

365 ἢ χρήματα ταῖς τῶν ἀντιπάλων ναυσὶν παρέχειν τινὰ πείθει,
ἢ κατατιλᾷ τῶν Ἑκαταίων κυκλίοισι χοροῖσιν ὑπᾴδων,
ἢ τοὺς μισθοὺς τῶν ποιητῶν ῥήτωρ ὢν εἶτ' ἀποτρώγει,
κωμῳδηθεὶς ἐν ταῖς πατρίοις τελεταῖς ταῖς τοῦ Διονύσου.
τούτοις αὐδῶ καὖθις ἐπαυδῶ καὖθις τὸ τρίτον μάλ' ἐπαυδῶ
370 ἐξίστασθαι μύσταισι χοροῖς· ὑμεῖς δ' ἀνεγείρετε μολπὴν
καὶ παννυχίδας τὰς ἡμετέρας αἳ τῇδε πρέπουσιν ἑορτῇ.

The chorus opens with a typical injunction against the uninitiated,[59] as a preparation for the iambic ode that will follow in 372-459. We have noted that when the ode begins, v. 372, the chorus makes it clear that they will sing a σκῶμμα. In the anapaests, that is, they demand that the audience be aware of the purpose of their invective. When they begin to list what kind of people they would exclude from their audience (those uninitiated into the "mysteries" of poetry in general and of Cratinus in particular, 356-57), Aristophanes reveals that he is concerned with the nature of the comic genre itself. At 357-68, the chorus spells out what amounts to a literary program. For it requires, first, that the audience understand (through a process of *initiation*) the particular style of Cratinus (μηδὲ Κρατίνου τοῦ ταυροφάγου γλώττης Βακχεῖ' ἐτελέσθη), and that they appreciate a certain refinement in comedy (ἢ βωμολόχοις ἔπεσιν χαίρει μὴ 'ν καιρῷ τοῦτο ποιοῦσιν).[60] Since, as we shall see in the next chapter, Cratinus was well known especially for the vehemence of his invective, when the chorus claims to want connoisseurs of Cratinean comedy as their audience, they imply, it seems, that such an audience would be more likely to appreciate their own abusive song.[61] The remaining anapaests bear this out. In 359-65 the chorus continues to describe their ideal audience, but now in political terms.[62] The injunctions are appropriate to the self-righteous pretence of comedy we discussed above, and show the chorus playing the role of the didactic

---

[59] Cf. Eurip. *Bacch.* 68-70 with Dodds' comments ad loc. p. 75, and Roux (1972) 266-67; also Kleinknecht (1937) 38ff.

[60] Σ RVE ad *Ran.* 357 claims that the epithet ταυροφάγος is used of Dionysus in a line in Sophocles' *Tyro* (cf. fr. 668 Radt), and it may reflect a cult title of the god. In any case, a "bull-eating tongue" applied to Cratinus must imply a vigorous poetic style. Cf. Stanford (1963) 106; also *Equ.* 526-28, where Aristophanes describes Cratinus' style metaphorically. His words, he says, could sweep away trees by their roots.

[61] The following line (358), in its disdain for poorly deployed silly jokes (ἢ βωμολόχοις ἔπεσιν χαίρει μὴ 'ν καιρῷ τοῦτο ποιοῦσιν), may also be intended to pay tribute to Cratinus' refinement of the genre, perhaps even his elevation of the cruder forms of the ἰαμβικὴ ἰδέα to a literary level in comedy.

[62] Again, as one would expect from a parabasis. Cf. Sifakis (1971) 39 (d1, d2).

comic poet. In 367-68 the chorus urges that politicians should stay away who, angered at being abused in the "ancestral festivals" (i.e. in comic drama, κωμῳδηθεὶς ἐν ταῖς πατρίοις τελεταῖς ταῖς τοῦ Διονύσου), diminish (i.e. "nibble away at," ἀποτρώγει) the rewards of the comic poet.[63] The participle κωμῳδηθείς is especially signficant since it firmly identifies κωμῳδία with the ritual abuse found in certain religious festivals. The juxtaposition of these two lines with the following (369-70: τούτοις αὐδῶ ... ἐξίστασθαι μύσταισι χοροῖς) implies that the kind of person who reacts aversely to being abused in comedy (a κωμῳδηθείς) would not understand the ritual-based invective of the song they proceed to sing. These lines, therefore, function as a defence of the abusiveness of comic drama, through an appeal to its religious background,[64] and the reenactment at 416ff. of a Gephyrismos-like ψόγος is not merely a gratuitous piece of humor, but offers also a religious sanction to the entire endeavor of Old Comedy.[65] The fact, then, that this ψόγος employs diction that has a distinct provenance in the literary Ionian iambos implies that this genre is considered an intermediate, "poetic" step in the development from ritual ψόγος to comic ψόγος.

A second Aristophanic passage that attests to the importance of the Ionian iambos for Old Comedy can be found in *Pax* 43-48:[66]

οὐκοῦν ἂν ἤδη τῶν θεατῶν τις λέγοι
νεανίας δοκησίσοφος· "τόδε πρᾶγμα τί;
45   ὁ κάνθαρος δὲ πρὸς τί;" κᾆτ' αὐτῷ γ' ἀνὴρ
Ἰωνικός τίς φησι παρακαθήμενος·
"δοκέω μέν, ἐς Κλέωνα τοῦτ' αἰνίσσεται,
ὡς κεῖνος ἀναιδέως τὴν σπατίλην ἐσθίει."

In 46 the servant of Trygaeus introduces an Ionian to explain to an Athenian why a dung beetle is on stage. Scholars have often wondered why an Ionian in particular should be brought on for this purpose. Platnauer

---

[63] Cf. Pickard-Cambridge (1962) 90, on the honorarium that seems to have been paid to the comic poet after he had been selected to compete.

[64] Cf. Stanford (1963) 107 ad 368: "Aristophanes emphasizes that the mockery on these occasions ... was not personal and malicious, but a traditional and essential part of venerable ceremonies."

[65] It is true that the chorus is composed of initiates and, as such, on one level they are justifying the abuse of their ritual, not necessarily of comedy. But it seems highly unlikely that Aristophanes, having just had the chorus refer to the invective of Cratinus (357) and to the abuse of individuals in the comic festivals (368), does not also make a connection between ritual abuse and comedy.

[66] This section, pp. 28-35 is a slightly abridged version of Rosen (1984).

concludes in *aporia*: "The *Peace* was produced at the City Dionysia, on which occasion foreigners were admitted into the theatre; otherwise there seems to be no particular reason for making this interlocutor an Ionian."⁶⁷ As Platnauer no doubt realized, the mere fact that foreigners were admitted to the City Dionysia hardly explains why an Ionian is specified at this point.

Sharpley offers what at first glance seems a plausible explanation: "sitting cheek by jowl . . . with the Athenian exquisite is an oracular philosopher from over the sea."⁶⁸ Although he elaborates no further, he evidently felt that the passage played on the contrast between an Athenian δοκησίσοφος (one who thinks he is σοφός) and an Ionian φιλόσοφος. Cassio shares this view and explains that in the passage "è adombrato un collegamento popolare tra intellettualità (o pretese d'intellettualità) e presenza di Ioni ad Atene."⁶⁹ On this interpretation, the servant implies that it takes an Ionian — i.e. a philosopher by nature — to appreciate the symbolism of the dung beetle. The passage, then, would function as a parody of philosophical explanation, since (1) the Ionian's rationalization degenerates into a scatological joke, and (2) the explanation is incorrect, for the dung beetle, as Aristophanes makes clear later on is *not* on stage primarily to ridicule Cleon (127ff., on which see below). Yet this approach seems only partially to explain the passage. It may be that the Ionian is meant to represent a typical intellectual,⁷⁰ but the details of his remarks seem intended to reveal a more specific characterization than this.

Van Leeuwen's comment that the Ionian represents a "provincialis aliqui homo,"⁷¹ though surely mistaken, nevertheless points to a better

---

⁶⁷ Platnauer (1964) 71 ad 46-48; on this point he echoes Blaydes (1883) 13 ad 46.
⁶⁸ Sharpley (1905) 62 ad 46.
⁶⁹ Cassio (1981) 91. Recently, Cassio (1985a) 105-6 has argued more elaborately that the passage is best explained in terms of what he sees as the larger political issues of the play, here specifically the criticism of the Athenians' behavior towards their Ionian colonies. The attack on Cleon in 46 by an Ionian, then, would highlight his especially harsh treatment of them. Cassio's interpretation of both the passage and the play overall is certainly compelling. As the discussion below indicates, however, I find at the same time that the passage also has other, non-political dimensions. In particular, the emphatic association of obscenity with an Ionian, as well as the fact that it is an Ionian who is called upon as an expert in animal fable, require exegesis.
⁷⁰ The popular conception of Ionians at Athens was that they were emasculated by their luxurious lifestyle. The references in comedy are almost unanimous on this; cf. for example, Callias fr. 8KA, Aristoph. *Pax* 929-36. While I can find no passage in extant fifth-century literature referring explicitly to Ionians as philosophers, Cassio (1981) 91 rightly points out that Ionian intellectualism was seen in Athens to be a consequence of their proverbial "softness." See especially Aristoph. *Equ.* 1375-80, where a sophistic discussion is imagined taking place in a perfume shop.
⁷¹ Van Leeuwen (1906) 16 ad 46.

approach. Van Leeuwen apparently felt that the Ionian's scatological joke (τὴν σπατίλην ἐσθίει) could only come from a crude and ill-bred individual. Although this contradicts the stereotypes of Ionians at the time, the premise that the obscenity is meant to seem appropriate to the Ionian's character is sound.[72] If we then ask what the connection is between scatological obscenity and Ionia, the answer must be the Ionian iambos. Because the prologue as a whole is designed to exploit the comic potential of the dung beetle's scatophagous habits, it seems likely that an Ionian is introduced at 46 precisely because of his presumed familiarity with this kind of humor. If Aristophanes associated (and expected his audience to associate) Ionia with the scatological (and sexual) αἰσχρολογία of the iambos, then the scatological joke in the mouth of an Ionian at 46 becomes eminently appropriate.[73] The fact that the Ionian's obscene explanation of the dung beetle amounts to an attack on Cleon, moreover, strengthens the connection with the iambos, in view of the iambographic use of αἰσχρολογία for invective purposes.[74] Although the joke at 46 exists solely for its attack on Cleon (ἐς Κλέωνα τοῦτ' αἰνίσσεται), part of its humor lies in the fact, as noted above, that the dung beetle does not function as a cipher for Cleon in the play as a whole. As Trygaeus states (129f), he chose the beetle because of its ability to fly to the gods, a notion he found ἐν τοῖσιν Αἰσώπου λόγοις. Therefore, as it is not Aristophanes' main purpose to ridicule Cleon through an allegorical dung beetle (as the Ionian supposes), the suggestion that an Ionian would nevertheless interpret the beetle along these lines parodies the willingness of an Ionian to see invective in anything.[75]

That the Ionian is meant to be seen as drawing on his knowledge of his native literary traditions becomes more certain when we consider that he is made to interpret the dung beetle as one would interpret an Ionian animal fable. That is, when he says that the beetle "is a riddle for/al-

---

[72] The fact that the servant quotes the Ionian in dialect suggests that he is concerned with verisimilitude of character. Van Herwerden (1897) 8 ad 45ff, compares the Ionian's function to that of the Megarians and Boeotians in *Acharnenses* who also speak in dialect, but concludes that in each instance the joke is simply that "plebeculae Atticae iocularis videbatur sermo hominum paullo aliter quam ipsi loquentium."

[73] Cf. *Eccl.* 883, where the old woman, in a hymnic parody, invokes the Muses for her "Ionian song" (μελύδριον . . . τῶν Ἰωνικῶν), which, as is clear from the ensuing amoebean song (900-23), implies αἰσχρολογία; cf. Ussher (1973) 196.

[74] E.g., Archilochus' frr. directed against the daughters of Lycambes (frr. 30-47W, esp. 42 and 43); Hipponax 69, 133Dg.

[75] It does also afford Aristophanes a fleeting attack on Cleon; but we must remember that Cleon had died the year before, and an extended diatribe against him (as in *Equ.* or *Vesp.*) would now have little point (as Trygaeus points out at 648-57).

ludes to" (αἰνίσσεται) Cleon's alleged scatophagy,[76] it seems that Aristophanes had in mind the derivation of the verb from the noun αἶνος, "animal fable."[77] Thus, αἰνίσσεται expresses the sentiment that the dung beetle is an ainos for Cleon. This becomes evident later in the prologue when Aristophanes explicitly acknowledges that he arrived at the idea of a dung beetle from Aesop (127-30):

> ΟΙ: τίς δ' ἠπίνοιά σούστὶν ὥστε κάνθαρον
> ζεύξαντ' ἐλαύνειν ἐς θεούς, ὦ πάππια;
> ΤΡ: ἐν τοῖσιν Αἰσώπου λόγοις ἐξηυρέθη
> μόνος πετηνῶν ἐς θεοὺς ἀφιγμένος.

As Trygaeus explains (on Aristophanes' behalf) at 133f, he had in mind specifically the fable of the Eagle and the Dung Beetle, and he refers to the part of the story where the beetle drops a ball of dung into Zeus' lap in an effort to dislodge the eagle's eggs that are lying there:[78] ἦλθεν κατ' ἔχθραν αἰετοῦ πάλαι ποτέ, ‖ ᾧ' ἐκκυλίνδων κἀντιτιμωρούμενος. Since, as this passage makes clear, the animal fable was represented in the fifth century most coherently by the distinctly Ionian Aesopic tradition,[79] it is especially appropriate at *Pax* 46 for an Ionian to see a fable allegory in the dung beetle.

That the ainos could be incorporated into the iambos as a vehicle of abuse (just as the Ionian of *Pax* views the dung beetle — an ainos "against Cleon") is shown by several Archilochian fragments. Thus fr. 174W begins:[80]

---

[76] For jokes involving scatophagy in Aristophanes see Henderson (1975) 192f.

[77] For the semantics of αἶνος see Nagy (1979) 237-40. Although the verb αἰνίσσομαι occurs in a variety of contexts, its predominant meaning of "saying one thing by means of another" seems to be derived from an original association with the Ionian ainos. Often the verb takes on an almost technical meaning involving the riddling of oracles (cf. Hdt. 5.56; Aristoph. *Equ.* 196, *Aves* 970; Plato *Apol.* 21b3). It is curious that all but the last of these passages involve animals in some way, perhaps preserving the original connection between αἰνίσσομαι and αἶνος as animal fable. On the interconnection between αἶνος / αἴνιγμα / αἰνίσσομαι see Nagy 240.

[78] See Perry (1952) 322 no. 3. Dung beetles also appear in no. 84 ("The Two Dung Beetles") and no. 112 ("The Ant and the Dung Beetle").

[79] On the animal fable as an originally Ionian genre cf. Hausrath *RE* 6 (1909) 1704-7 s. v. "Fabel." On the Oriental origins of the fable tradition see Perry (1965) xix-xxxiv. Aesop came (according to the most reliable accounts) from the Ionian island of Samos, where he would no doubt have come into contact with Eastern fable traditions; on Aesop's life cf. Perry (1965) xxxv ff.

[80] For the fragments associated with ainoi, see West (1971), frr. 172-81, 185-87, with p. 64 for the ancient testimonia about Archilochus' use of the animal fable. See also Burnett (1983) 60-66.

> αἶνός τις ἀνθρώπων ὅδε,
> ὡς ἄρ' ἀλώπηξ καἰετὸς ξυνεωνίην
> ἔμειξαν,

and if editors are right to place it among the Lycambes poems (172-81W), this fragment helps to fulfill the promise of 172W: πάτερ Λυκάμβα . . . νῦν δὲ δὴ πολὺς ‖ ἀστοῖσι φαίνεαι γέλως. Elsewhere (185W) Archilochus employed in a similar fashion[81] the fable of the fox and the monkey:

> ἐρέω τιν' ὕμιν αἶνον, ὦ Κηρυκίδη,
> ἀχνυμένῃ σκυτάλῃ,
> πίθηκος ᾔει θηρίων ἀποκριθεὶς
> μοῦνος ἀν' ἐσχατιήν,
> τῷ δ' ἄρ' ἀλώπηξ κερδαλῆ συνήντετο,
> πυκνὸν ἔχουσα νόον.

The numerous testimonia concerning this fragment collected by West indicate that this particular treatment of the fable was well known in antiquity, and that by the fifth century the ainos had become closely associated with the most prominent iambographer.[82] This, in turn, helps to explain more fully why an Ionian is introduced in the *Pax* passage: someone from Ionia who would be sensitive to both the iambos and the ainos (and their apparent interaction) would quickly assume that the dung beetle on the stage, because of its scatophagous habits, must be intended as an allegorical attack on someone.

Two passages in Aristophanes' *Vespae* in fact indicate a fifth-century awareness of the use of the fable for invective. Having been advised by his son that quoting Aesop is a mark of social refinement (1259), Philocleon tries his hand at it with the baking woman. In a humorous misinterpretation of Bdelycleon's original advice — to tell something amusing from Aesop (Αἰσωπικὸν γέλοιον) — Philocleon begins to tell a

---

[81] As Lasserre (1950) 131 points out, the phrase ἐρέω + vocative implies that the fable is addressed to someone and that its lesson will be directed at that person. (His reconstruction of the details of the epode, however, is highly speculative).

[82] In one of Plato's few references to Archilochus, for example, Adeimantus alludes to the fable (*Resp.* 363c, τὴν δὲ . . . Ἀρχιλόχου ἀλωπέκα . . . κερδαλέαν καὶ ποικίλην. Cf. also Pindar *Pyth.* 2.76-78, which speaks of διαβολιᾶν ὑποφάτιες, ‖ ὀργαῖς ἀτενὲς ἀλωπέκων ἴκελοι. That this alludes to the Archilochian fable is suggested by the fact that the iambographer is given programmatic status earlier in the ode, (see above p. 13, and further in Rosen [1984] 393 n. 16).

story *about* Aesop. Nevertheless, he makes his story reflect the fact that Aesop was a fabulist, and it becomes a kind of fable in itself (1401-5):

> Αἴσωπον ἀπὸ δείπνου βαδίζονθ᾽ ἑσπέρας
> θρασεῖα καὶ μεθύση τις ὑλάκτει κύων.
> κἄπειτ᾽ ἐκεῖνος εἶπεν· "ὦ κύον, κύον,
> εἰ νὴ Δί᾽ ἀντὶ τῆς κακῆς γλώττης ποθὲν
> πυροὺς πρίαιο, σωφρονεῖν ἄν μοι δοκεῖς."

It is clear that the story is here meant to refer to Philocleon and the baking woman, where Philocleon is Aesop and the baking woman is the barking dog. The baking woman realizes too that this "Aesopic" story is directed against her, as her reply demonstrates: καὶ καταγελᾷς μου;

At 1446, Philocleon, still determined to take Bdelycleon's advice, begins another story about Aesop:

ΦΙ: Αἴσωπον οἱ Δελφοί ποτ᾽ —
ΒΔ: ὀλίγον μοι μέλει.
ΦΙ: φιάλην ἐπῃτιῶντο κλέψαι τοῦ θεοῦ.
      ὁ δ᾽ ἔλεξεν αὐτοῖς ὡς ὁ κάνθαρός ποτε —

The story, preserved in the biographical tradition, relates that Aesop was unjustly accused by the Delphians of stealing a sacred bowl and condemned to death;[83] before his death, he told an ainos to the Delphians as a way of illustrating their folly. Some versions[84] say that he told the fable of the Eagle and the Dung Beetle. Philocleon here makes Aesop use this fable as a pointed attack on the Delphians, which reveals his awareness that the fable is an appropriate vehicle for such a purpose.[85] His use of the dung beetle, moreover, implies that the fifth-century Athenian would naturally associate this creature with Aesop, and it thus affirms further the Aesopic background of the dung beetle in *Pax*.

If we can next show that Aristophanes himself was aware that the scatological humor of the entire *Pax* prologue was akin to, if not derived from, the conventions of the Ionian iambos, then our explanation of the Ionian's function at 46 becomes even more probable. To this end we may turn to Hipponax fr. 95.7-13Dg:[86]

---

[83] See Wiechers (1961).
[84] E. g., Vitae G/W 134-39, Perry (1952) 76f., 106f.
[85] For the Aesopic ainos as a vehicle for blame, see Nagy (1979) 281-83.
[86] For a discussion of the context of this fragment (probably a description of a ritual for retrieving someone's sexual virility) see Latte (1929) and Masson (1962) 150.

ἥ τε ⌊κρ⌋ά⌊δ⌋η με τούτέρωθ[εν
ἄνω⌊θεν ἐ⌋μ⌊ι⌋πίπτο⌊υσα, κ[
πα⌊ραψι{δ}ά⌋ζω⌊ι⌋ν βολ⌊βίτῳ [
10 ὦζεν δὲ λαύρη· κάνθαρο⌊ι δὲ ῥοιζέοντες
ἦλθον κατ' ὀδμὴν πλέον⌊ες ἢ πεντήκοντα·
τῶν οἱ μὲν ἐμπίπτοντε[ς
κατέβαλον . . .

Henderson (1975) 23 has remarked that the detail of "over fifty dung beetles . . . swarming in a squadron toward the latrine . . . distinctly foreshadows the prologue to *Peace*." In particular, Trygaeus' paratragic speech at 149ff. does seem to be a deliberate development of the comic ramifications of the Hipponactean scene. In Hipponax, the swarm of beetles apparently attacks the speaker, attracted to the smell of the βόλβιτος (ἦλθον κατ' ὀδμὴν). At 151ff. Trygaeus, riding on the back of one of these creatures, imagines a similar situation and pleads with the men at Athens:

μὴ βδεῖτε μηδὲ χέζεθ' ἡμερῶν τριῶν·
ὡς εἰ μετέωρος οὗτος ὢν ὀσφρήσεται,
κατωκάρα ῥίψας με βουκολήσεται.

When the beetle begins to veer towards earth, Trygaeus says (157f): ποῖ παρακλίνεις ‖ τοὺς μυκτῆρας πρὸς τὰς λαύρας; to which we may compare v. 10 of the Hipponax fragment, ὦζεν δὲ λαύρη.

It is true, as noted above, that Aristophanes claims to have derived the dung beetle from Aesop (127ff.), and he certainly makes no mention of Hipponax in the prologue. Yet his own use of the fable owes much more, it seems, to the kind of scatological humor found in the Hipponax fragment than to the original Aesopic version.[87] It seems, therefore, that Aristophanes was conscious of the Ionian literary provenance of the scatological jokes concerned with the dung beetle, and consequently it is easy to understand why at 46 an Ionian is chosen to engage in this sort of humor.[88]

---

[87] For other scatological references in the iambographers cf. Henderson (1975) 22. In the prologue to *Pax* note the details of 99-101 (κοπρῶνες, λαῦραι, πρωκτοὺς ἐπικλείειν) and 162-65, which are more in the spirit of the Hipponax fragment than of Aesop.

[88] We may note that the expression σπατίλην ἐσθίει put into the mouth of the Ionian (48) also suggests that he is meant to be drawing on his acquaintance with the iambos. For rather than a common word for excrement (such as σκῶρ, βόλβιτος, or κόπρος; cf.

Henderson 192-94), he chooses σπατίλη ("diarrhea"), a rare Ionic word which, apart from its comic usage here, appears only as a medical term (as in the Hippocratic *De Diaeta Acutorum* 28; for other instances cf. Herwerden [1897] 9). Used of Cleon, the term is a particularly clever choice, since, as Henderson (1975) 192 points out, it plays on the leather (σπάτος) associated with his tanning profession and τιλᾶν ("to excrete"). This does not, of course, alter the fact that it would have had a distinctly Ionian ring to the Athenian audience. Since it is apparent from the fragments that the iambographers were fond of this kind of technical vocabulary for comic purposes (see further Rosen [1984] 396 n. 26), the use of the word σπατίλη at 48 would be appropriate for an Ionian trying to parade his familiarity with iambographic diction.

CHAPTER III
CRATINUS

The evidence we have examined above suggests that the Athenian comic poets were aware of both the distinguishing poetic features of the Ionian iambos and the appropriateness of these features to their own genre. This awareness, moreover, reflected their realization that the satirical and antagonistic elements of their plays derived from an impulse fundamentally similar to that of the iambic ψόγος. The questions that remain are these: When did the Athenian comic poets begin to exploit the affinities between the two genres? Can it be considered a distinct literary movement within the development of Old Comedy?

If we were left only with the evidence of Aristophanes' plays, we would be tempted to conclude that he alone was responsible for importing *ad hominem* abuse into comedy, and elevating it to a literary level. At *Pax* 750f, for example, Aristophanes implies that his abusive approach is something of an innovation when the coryphaeus boasts that the poet attacks important men such as Cleon, while his rivals restrict themselves to more common citizens (ἰδιώτας ἀνθρωπίσκους). Elsewhere, too, Aristophanes boasts that he was the first one to engage in bold, personal abuse serving didactic purposes.[1] But in spite of such claims to originality, Cratinus, composing in the decades before Aristophanes' first production, has been recognized as the pivotal figure in the development of the ἰαμβικὴ ἰδέα. As Schmid states, with Cratinus "sollte nicht mehr nur mit albernen Possenreissereien belustigen, sondern durch Tadel, Spott, persönlichen Angriff auf die Schuldigen dem Staat zu Nutzen reden, für die σωτηρία τῆς πόλεως sorgen."[2] To this figure we may now turn our attention.

Few details are certain about the chronology of Cratinus' life and career. From the list of comic victors at the City Dionysia (IG II/III² 2.2325 col. I.50 = Cratinus Test. 5KA), Cratinus' first victory is dated to approximately 456 (certainly no earlier).[3] In Aristophanes' *Equites* 526-

---

[1] Cf. Sifakis (1971) 39 (c1) for other such boasts in Aristophanes.
[2] Schmid (1946) 10.
[3] Cratinus is listed two places after Euphronius, the victor for 458 B.C. Cf. Körte (1922) 1647, and Pickard-Cambridge (1968) 112, 116. On the dating of *Archilochoi*, which has often been considered Cratinus' earliest extant play, see below nn. 18, 35.

36 (produced in 424) Cratinus is represented as an old man (532). The testimony of *Pax* 700 (produced 421), which claimed that Cratinus had died the year before "when the Laconians invaded," remains an enigma. Most scholars agree that this passage cannot refer to the poet's actual death, since no Spartan invasion is recorded for that year, but whether Aristophanes meant to imply that Cratinus' creative powers were waning remains uncertain.[4] Still, the evidence we do have makes it likely that Cratinus was poetically active from the 450's through the 420's,[5] and no doubt the peak of his creativity fell squarely in the 440's.

The first indication of Cratinus' great importance in the development of the ἰαμβικὴ ἰδέα of Old Comedy occurs in Aristophanes *Equites* 526-36, where the coryphaeus, lamenting the difficulties of being a comic poet, offers a summary history of the genre up to his time:

εἶτα Κρατίνου μεμνημένος, ὃς πολλῷ ῥεύσας ποτ' ἐπαίνῳ
διὰ τῶν ἀφελῶν πεδίων ἔρρει, καὶ τῆς στάσεως παρασύρων
ἐφόρει τὰς δρῦς καὶ τὰς πλατάνους καὶ τοὺς ἐχθροὺς προθε-
    λύμνους·
ᾆσαι δ' οὐκ ἦν ἐν συμποσίῳ πλὴν· Δωροῖ συκοπέδιλε,
530 καὶ τέκτονες εὐπαλάμων ὕμνων· οὕτως ἤνθησεν ἐκεῖνος.
νυνὶ δ' ὑμεῖς αὐτὸν ὁρῶντες παραληροῦντ' οὐκ ἐλεεῖτε,
ἐκπιπτουσῶν τῶν ἠλέκτρων καὶ τοῦ τόνου οὐκέτ' ἐνόντος
τῶν θ' ἁρμονιῶν διαχασκουσῶν· ἀλλὰ γέρων ὢν περιέρρει,
ὥσπερ Κοννᾶς, στέφανον μὲν ἔχων αὖον, δίψῃ δ' ἀπολωλώς,
535 ὃν χρῆν διὰ τὰς προτέρας νίκας πίνειν ἐν τῷ πρυτανείῳ,
καὶ μὴ ληρεῖν, ἀλλὰ θεᾶσθαι λιπαρὸν παρὰ τῷ Διονύσῳ.

Cratinus appears here as the second of a trio representing the prevalent styles of contemporary comedy: Magnes (vv. 520-25), Cratinus, and Crates (vv. 537-40).[6] In the case of Cratinus, the image of the uncontrollable

---

[4] As, for example, Schwarze (1971) 6. See also Platnauer (1964) 127 ad 700-3.

[5] According to Σ *Equ.* 531, Cratinus was outraged at Aristophanes for portraying him as a hopeless drunk at the Lenaea of 424 (*Equ.* 531), and so retaliated at the City Dionysia of 423 by accusing him in *Pytine* of plagiarizing Eupolis. (*Pytine* won first prize over *Nubes*.) Aristophanes referred to Cratinus' drunkenness as late as 421 (cf. *Pax* 702f). See also Körte (1922) col. 1647ff.

[6] See Neil (1901) 81 ad 537: "The three poets are well chosen to mark different styles and stages of their art, Magnes the comedy of the old folk or beast tale, Cratinus the Old Comedy of personal attack, Crates a foreshadowing of New Comedy." On Magnes, see Pickard-Cambridge (1962) 189-91; the few titles we have of his plays suggest that he was fond of animal choruses, e.g., "Fish-flies," "Frogs," "Birds." On animal choruses, see Sifakis (1971) 73-102.

river flooding the plains and wrenching out everything in its path implies that his stylistic distinction lay in the peculiar strength of his language. When Aristophanes mentions that Cratinus was much praised for his imposing style (ὃς πολλῷ ῥεύσας ποτ' ἐπαίνῳ, 526)[7] he seems to indicate that this style was novel at the time (why else bother to mention audience approval in this context?).[8] The next two lines indicate that the strong language Aristophanes has in mind is invective: "as he was sweeping[9] over the plains, he carried away from their foundation oaks, plane trees, καὶ τοὺς ἐχθροὺς προθελύμνους." This *paraprosdokian*, which intrudes upon the river metaphor, characterizes Cratinus' concerns as essentially abusive, and the subsequent lines attest to the popularity of this type of comedy. It appears to have been fashionable, for example, to recite on social occasions such lines of invective as Δωροῖ συκοπέδιλε (529).[10] Apparently, Cratinus liked this characterization of his style, for in the following year we find these lines (fr. 198KA from *Pytine*):[11]

> ἄναξ Ἄπολλον, τῶν ἐπῶν τοῦ ῥεύματος,
> καναχοῦσι πηγαί· δωδεκάκρουνον <τὸ> στόμα,
> Ἰλισὸς ἐν τῇ φάρυγι. τί ἂν εἴποιμ' <ἔτι>;
> εἰ μὴ γὰρ ἐπιβύσει τις αὐτοῦ τὸ στόμα,
> 5 ἅπαντα ταῦτα κατακλύσει ποιήμασιν

That Cratinus refers to his own poetry as a "cataclysm of poetry" (5) shows both a distinct literary self-consciousness and a sense of pride in

---

[7] On ῥέω as applied to the flow of words, cf. *LSJ* s.v. 2. Note also Horace's description of Pindar at *Carm.* 4.2.5-8.

[8] Much later, Persius may have had this in mind when he called Cratinus *audax* at *Sat.* 1.123: *audaci quicumque adflato Cratino*.

[9] Ps.-Longinus *de Subl.* 33.5 uses this verb (παρασύρω) with reference to Archilochus (= Tarditi Test. 14): τί δέ; Ἐρατοσθένης ἐν τῇ Ἠριγόνῃ ... Ἀρχιλόχου πολλὰ καὶ ἀνοικονόμητα παρασύροντος, κἀκείνης τῆς ἐκβολῆς τοῦ δαιμονίου πνεύματος ... ἆρα δὴ μείζων ποιητής; The use of παρασύρω in both cases as a literary-critical term shows that both Archilochus and Cratinus had styles that were considered "forceful" in antiquity. The river image is used again by Horace of Pindar's language (cf. above n. 7).

[10] Cf. Σ ad *Equ.* 529: Κρατίνου μέλους ἀρχή· σκώπτων δέ τινα ἐκεῖνος δωροδόκον καὶ συκοφάντην τοῦτο εἶπε, and Blaydes (1892) 302 ad 529. Note here the comic vocative formed from the word for "fig" (σῦκον) and "sandal" (πέδιλον); i.e. "Goddess Bribery, fig-sandaled," a parody of epic epithets (Homer has χρυσοπέδιλος of Hera at *Od.* 11.604) with a pun, it seems, on σῦκον and συκοφάντης.

[11] On this play cf. above n. 5. Σ *Equ.* 526 says Κρατῖνος περὶ αὑτοῦ μεγαληγορῶν, and Kock I.70 remarks: "de Cratino haec nescio quis dicit; sed utrum in iudicio amicorum an postquam cum comoedia in gratiam rediit, incertum est." Note that the scholiast has his chronology wrong when he goes on to say that Aristophanes got his idea of the river metaphor from Cratinus' lines.

his particular stylistic achievements. In the light of this passage, it seems all the more likely that Aristophanes' epithet for Cratinus, ταυροφάγος, at *Ranae* 357 alludes, as is often suggested, to the poet's style (see above, p. 27 n. 60). For Aristophanes, it seems, Cratinus was the quintessential representative of κωμῳδεῖν ὀνομαστί, and we may infer from the fact that the *Equites* passage purports to offer a literary history that Aristophanes considered Cratinus as one of the first (if not *the* first) to innovate in this direction.

Some of the most important indirect testimonia about Cratinus come from the excerpts of Platonius' commentary on Aristophanes. These excerpts, preserved in several Aristophanes manuscripts and apparently of reliable lineage,[12] offer the earliest explicitly literary-critical appraisal of Cratinus after Aristophanes, and agree with our conclusions drawn above from the portrait in *Equites*:

Κρατῖνος ὁ τῆς παλαιᾶς κωμῳδίας ποιητής, ἅτε δὴ κατὰ τὰς Ἀρχιλόχου ζηλώσεις,[13] αὐστηρὸς μὲν ταῖς λοιδορίαις ἐστίν· οὐ γάρ, ὥσπερ Ἀριστοφάνης, ἐπιτρέχειν τὴν χάριν τοῖς σκώμμασι ποιεῖ τὸ φορτικὸν τῆς ἐπιτιμήσεως διὰ ταύτης ἀναιρῶν, ἀλλ' ἁπλῶς κατὰ τὴν παροιμίαν "γυμνῇ τῇ κεφαλῇ" τίθησι τὰς βλασφημίας κατὰ τῶν ἁμαρτανόντων. πολὺς δὲ καὶ <ἐν> ταῖς τροπαῖς τυγχάνει. εὔστοχος δὲ ὢν ἐν ταῖς ἐπιβολαῖς τῶν δραμάτων καὶ διασκευαῖς, εἶτα προϊὼν καὶ διασπῶν τὰς ὑποθέσεις οὐκ ἀκολούθως πληροῖ τὰ δράματα. (Koster II.1-8 = Cratinus Test. 17KA)

Platonius states that Cratinus was a literary follower of Archilochus, and hence "severe in his wranglings." He means, of course, that because (ἅτε) Cratinus emulated Archilochus, personal abuse played a prominent role in his drama. Cratinus is characterized as relentlessly abusive

---

[12] See Kaibel (1899) 1 n. 1, and Koster II.3. The excerpts are in two parts: περὶ διαφορᾶς κωμῳδιῶν and περὶ διαφορᾶς χαρακτήρων. Wendel (1950) col. 2544 says, "Der Umstand, dass im ersten Abschnitt die νέα nur beiläufig erwähnt wird, ohne die Definition der Komödie und die Unterscheidungsmerkmale der παλαιά und μέση mitzubestimmen, sowie die feine, an Dionysios von Halikarnass und Quintilian bzw. deren Vorlage erinnernde Vergleichung der drei Komödiendichter im zweiten Abschnitt *weisen darauf hin dass P. eine sehr alte Quelle benutzt hat* [my emphasis]." This is an extremely important point — not stressed by most scholars — since Platonius' comments about Cratinus are often assumed without question to be correct.

[13] The emendation of Hemsterhuis (*apud* Geel [1828] 8), ἅτε δὴ καὶ τὰ Ἀρχιλόχου ζηλώσας, has been endorsed recently by Marzullo (1982). The meaning in either case is essentially the same.

in contrast to Aristophanes, who at least softened his invective with a certain amount of χάρις. Insofar as Cratinus "reviled malefactors with singular intent" (ἁπλῶς . . . τίθησι τὰς βλασφημίας κατὰ τῶν ἁμαρτανόντων), Platonius sees him as engaging in the same activity as Archilochus.[14] Elsewhere in Platonius (Koster II.15 = Test. 17KA), Cratinus is described as πικρὸς λίαν and as having a "sternness against malefactors" (πρὸς τοὺς ἁμαρτανόντας τὸ σφοδρόν), both of which judgments were applied in antiquity to the iambographers.[15]

In another late treatise, the anonymous *De Comoedia*, we find a passage (Koster V.15ff. = Cratinus Test. 19KA) which explicitly acknowledges Cratinus' interest in developing the pretence of moral amelioration through violent invective: . . . καὶ τῷ χαρίεντι τῆς κωμῳδίας τὸ ὠφέλιμον προσέθηκε, τοὺς κακῶς πράσσοντας διαβάλλων καὶ ὥσπερ δημοσίᾳ μάστιγι τῇ κωμῳδίᾳ κολάζων.[16]

The above testimonia offer a clear and uniform picture of Cratinus' contribution to comedy. They imply that he was the first comic poet to attend to literary style, and to have articulated to subsequent comic poets a self-consciousness about the genre. This style, moreover, which is alleged to owe its inspiration to the iambos (ἅτε δὴ κατὰ τὰς Ἀρχιλόχου ζηλώσεις) embraced the element of κωμῳδεῖν ὀνομαστί that would become further refined in the hands of Aristophanes.[17] So far, however,

---

[14] We may recall that Alcidamas (=Tarditi Test. 6) referred to Archilochus as βλάσφημος (see above pp. 13-14).

[15] Note, for example, Oenomaus ap. Euseb. *Praep. Evang.* 5.32-39 (= Tarditi Test. 115), who says of Archilochus: λοιδορῆσαι μὲν πικρῶς τὰς οὐκ ἐθελούσας ἡμῖν γαμεῖσθαι. We should not overlook the fact that Platonius also claims (Cratinus p. 192 KA = Koster I.30 and 51) that Cratinus composed mythological burlesque in a Middle Comedy vein, as in his *Odysseis*, which "contained no personal attack, but rather parody (διασυρμόν) of the *Odyssey*." It is true that mythological burlesques were prevalent in Old Comedy, but the nature of such plays is not well known. As we shall see below, even Cratinus' mythological burlesques could be used as vehicles of abuse. See pp. 49-57.

[16] This passage also mentions that Cratinus was the first to introduce the third actor to comedy. Since Aristotle (*Poet.* 1449b4) states that no one knew who was the first to do this, the reliability of the testimony about Cratinus has been questioned (Körte [1922] col. 1650 deemed it "worthless"). But the claim that Cratinus first introduced three actors could be an erroneous inference from the combination of the fact that three actors appeared in some of his plays, and that he was perhaps the earliest Athenian comic poet known to the commentator. This mistake, in short, need not destroy the credibility of the literary-critical judgment that follows it.

[17] The anonymous author of the *De Com.* (Cratinus Test. 2a.10 KA = Koster III.24) calls Cratinus . . . ποιητικώτατος, κατασκευάζων εἰς τὸν Αἰσχύλου χαρακτῆρα. By ποιητικώτατος he seems to mean that Cratinus paid close attention to the poetic craft of comedy, and was attuned to the influences of other poetic traditions on his own (such as Aeschylus', as we see from this passage; or Archilochus', as ἅτε δὴ κατὰ τὰς Ἀρχιλόχου ζηλώσεις, in the passage previously cited, shows).

the explicit evidence we have examined for the influence of the iambos on Cratinus is indirect and somewhat late, and if this were all we had, there would still remain cause for uncertainty. Fortunately, when we turn to the extant fragments, we find that they offer a portrait of Cratinus consonant with that which emerges from the testimonia.

We may begin, appropriately enough, with *Archilochoi*.[18] The title alone, of course, is sufficient to indicate that Cratinus had some interest in the Parian iambographer, although the details of the plot are unclear. It is almost certain, however, that the chorus consisted of Archilochus and his followers.[19] The few fragments we possess from this play, moreover, attest that it had something to do with the Archilochian poetic. Fr. 6KA, for example, seems to refer explicitly to Archilochian poetry, and although the context is uncertain, we may be fairly certain that Archilochus is here being praised:

εἶδες τὴν Θασίαν ἅλμην, οἷ᾽ ἄττα βαΰζει;
ὡς εὖ καὶ ταχέως ἀπετείσατο καὶ παραχρῆμα.
οὐ μέντοι παρὰ κωφὸν ὁ τυφλὸς ἔοικε λαλῆσαι

Meineke first explained this fragment by suggesting that Θασίαν ἅλμην refers simultaneously to Archilochus' stay in Thasos and his notorious poetic acerbity: "Thasian brine" = Archilochian poetry.[20] Some scholars have supposed that the fragment implies that Archilochus appears on the stage (the chorus, in this case, would be referring to this

---

[18] For most of this century, scholars generally regarded *Archilochoi* as the earliest attested play by Cratìnus. Its date rested primarily on fr. 1.5-6KA, which alludes to the recent death of Cimon (ὁ δὲ λιπών ‖ βέβηκε πρότερος). The reference to Cimon's death has been felt to be "of such an intimate nature that it would be timely only within a short time after the death of the admired statesman" (Tanner [1920] 173, endorsing Bergk [1838] 20). Since Cimon died in 450 or 449, the production of *Archilochoi* was dated to c. 449. See Kock I.11; Schwarze (1971) 83 n. 210, and 87. Luppe (1966) 136-37 and (1973) 124-27, however, has emphasized how subjective this conclusion really is. We can conclude little more from it, he argues, than that 449 is a *terminus post quem* for *Archilochoi*. On the whole question of the dating of this play see below n. 35.

[19] See Kock I.11; Bergk (1838) 4-5, who cites examples of referring to disciples by the plural name, e.g., Aristoph. *Aves* 1701, Γοργίαι τε καὶ Φίλιπποι ("followers of Gorgias and Philippus"). See also Schwarze (1971) 79, n. 195.

[20] Meineke II.i.17: "de homine salso et amari ingenii, quemadmodum Ἀλμίωνος nomen ad ingenii acerbitatem referebatur." For a complete list of references to Thasos in Archilochus, see Schwarze (1971) 79, n. 193. See also Pretagostini (1982), who suggests that "Thasian brine" also refers to a culinary practice of dipping a fish into brine after it has been grilled on charcoal; hence the victim of Archilochian πικρία emerges "grilled" like a fish.

with εἶδες τὴν Θασίαν ἅλμην),²¹ although, without further evidence as to the context, Schwarze's explanation, (1971) 80 n. 197, has equal force: "hier kann es sich auch um eine einzelne Reminiszenz handeln, derart, dass die Choreuten, die ja als Zeitgenossen des parischer Dichters figurieren, von einem Vertreter des gegenwärtigen Athen über ihr Idol ausgefragt werden." At any rate, we may be sure that the play was somehow concerned with types of poetry, perhaps dramatizing a contest between Archilochian (i.e. iambographic) and epic poets (as represented perhaps by two half-choruses).²² The fragment does imply in v. 2 that Archilochus was responding to a previous speaker (ὡς εὖ καὶ ταχέως ἀπετείσατο καὶ παραχρῆμα) and, typical of an iambographer, his response is viewed as a requital (an ἀπότισις) for a perceived injustice against him.²³ Fr. 2KA also suggests that *Archilochoi* presented a literary agon: οἷον σοφιστῶν σμῆνος ἀνεδιφήσατε (from Diog. Laert. *Proem.* 12: καὶ οἱ ποιηταὶ [ἐκαλοῦντο] σοφισταί, καθὰ καὶ Κρατῖνος ἐν ' Ἀρχιλόχοις τοὺς περὶ ῞Ομηρον καὶ ῾Ησίοδον ἐπαινῶν οὕτως καλεῖ).²⁴ In view of Cratinus' own iambic proclivities, it is likely that his own sympathies lay with the chorus (or the half-chorus that represented Archilochus). Since, as our testimonia imply, Cratinus was the first to refine the abusive element that became so popular in Old Comedy through a deliberate emulation of Archilochus, it is likely that *Archilochoi* was composed with the intention of legitimizing this approach to comedy.

Other fragments from *Archilochoi* give us some idea of how Cratinus incorporated iambographic elements into his plays. Fr. 11KA, for

---

²¹ Körte (1922) col. 1650f; Kock I.13.
²² Körte (1922) col. 1651; along these lines Whittaker (1935) 185, suggests that the chorus is divided into two as in *Ach.* and *Lys.*, the one half supporting the epic poets, the other Archilochus. Whittaker would, therefore, assign Cratinus 6KA to the antode of the agon: "In Aristophanic agones the antagonist who is destined to lose the contest always begins the epirrhema, while the agonist begins the antepirrhema. In this case it is unthinkable that Archilochus, Cratinus' model, should be defeated, so presumably Homer [= ὁ τυφλός, v. 3] as potential victim opened the agon."
²³ Cf. Archil. fr. 104 Tarditi (= 126W): ἓν δ' ἐπίσταμαι μέγα ‖ τὸν κακῶς <μ'> ἔρδοντα δέννοισ' ἀνταμείβεσθαι κακοῖς, where ἀνταμείβεσθαι corresponds to ἀπετείσατο.
²⁴ See Meineke II.i.16 for other examples from Old Comedy where poets are referred to as "sophists." The verb ἀναδιφάω is glossed by *LSJ* as "grope after." The uncompounded διφάω, however, means "to search after," usually in contexts where the area is a vast unknown, e.g., the heavens, the sea (as in Homer *Il.* 16.747). Cf. Aristoph. *Nub.* 192: οὗτοι δ' ἐρεβοδιφῶσιν ὑπὸ τὸν Τάρταρον. Cratinus 2KA, therefore, may refer to "searching out (and dredging up, ἀνα-)" a swarm of poets from the underworld.

example, contains an unmistakable allusion to Archilochus fr. 168W:[25]

Ἐρασμονίδη Βάθιππε τῶν ἀωρολείων (fr. 11KA)
Ἐρασμονίδη Χαρίλαε,
χρῆμά τοι γελοῖον
ἐρέω, πολὺ φίλταθ᾽ ἑταίρων,
τέρψεαι δ᾽ ἀκούων. (Archil. fr. 168W)

It has long been recognized that the patronymic Ἐρασμονίδη in Cratinus is not used because Bathippus' father was actually named "Erasmon," but rather because it ridicules Bathippus' lustful nature.[26] This type of comic patronymic, of course, was common in the iambic poets and abounds in Aristophanes.[27] Cratinus' use of an Archilochian comic patronymic, it seems, acknowledges a similarity between their aims and methods as invective poets.

Hephaestion at *Enchir.* 15.1ff. claims that Cratinus consciously adapted the metrical components of the asynartetic cola found in Archilochus fr. 168W.[28] As an example of this he quotes Cratinus fr. 360KA, the first two lines of which differ slightly from Archilochus in that their colon division occurs a syllable earlier.[29] As we have seen, fr. 11KA leaves little doubt that Cratinus was familar with Archilochus fr. 168W, and this makes it all the more likely that Hephaestion was correct when he says that Cratinus used the Archilochian line as a metrical model for fr. 360KA.[30] Although Cratinus' version of Archilochian asynarteta ap-

---

[25] This fragment is especially resonant; it is indebted to Homer (Tarditi compares v. 2 with *Od.* 24.517 and *Il.* 1.474), and, in turn, it inspired Catullus 56.1-2: *o rem ridiculam, Cato, et iocosam* ‖ *dignamque auribus et tuo cachinno.*

[26] Meineke I.22; Kock I.15.

[27] Kock cites, for example, Aristoph. *Ach.* 595-97 with its three consecutive line endings: σπουδαρχίδης ... στρατωνίδης ... μισθαρχίδης. See also Bonanno (1980), esp. 74-79.

[28] The "anapaestic hephthemimer" (as Heph. calls it), here =
x – ⏑ ⏑ – ⏑ ⏑ – –
and the ithyphallic, here =
– ⏑ ⏑⏑ ⏑ – – .

On Archilochian asynarteta, see Rossi (1976) 207-229. For a different view, cf. West (1982) 43.

[29] χαῖρ᾽, ὦ μέγ᾽ ἀχρειόγελως ὅμιλε ταῖς ἐπίβδαις,
τῆς ἡμετέρας σοφίας κριτὴς ἄριστε πάντων·
εὐδαίμον᾽ ἔτικτέ σε μήτηρ ἰκρίων ψόφησις.

Hephaestion's point is that Cratinus deviated from the Archilochian asynarteta in his indifference to colon division.

[30] It is interesting that Hephaestion does in fact mention fr. 11KA (Ἐρασμονίδη Βάθιππε τῶν ἀωρολείων) at *Enchir.* 15.8, but only to say that "Cratinus in *Archilochoi* made a mistake with [ἀγνοεῖ] this meter [the asynarteta], because he does not imitate

pears also in other comic poets,³¹ Cratinus is the earliest poet to use it, and it is probable that his own great interest in Archilochus prompted his metrical innovation.

Frr. 12 + 81KA offer further insight into the influence of the iambos on Cratinus. The two frr. actually derive from the same source, Σ Lucian *Iup. Trag.* 48, but are separated by Kassel-Austin because the scholiast seems to refer to two of Cratinus' plays, *Archilochoi* and *Thraittai*:³²

ὁ μὲν Καλλίας οὗτος, ὡς Κρατῖνος 'Αρχιλόχοις φησίν, 'Ιππονίκου υἱὸς ἦν, τὸν δῆμον Μελιτεύς, ὡς 'Αριστοφάνης "Ωραις, πλούσιος καὶ πασχητιῶν καὶ ὑπὸ πορνιδίων διαφορούμενος καὶ κόλακας τρέφων. (fr. 12KA)

εἰς δὲ στιγματίαν αὐτὸν Κρατῖνος κωμῳδεῖ ὡς ἕνα τῶν κατάχρεων Θρᾴτταις (θρᾶττες Δ, corr. Luppe, om. V) . . . κωμῳδεῖ δὲ αὐτὸν Κρατῖνος καὶ ὡς Φώκου γυναῖκα μοιχεύσαντα καὶ τρία τάλαντα δόντα εἰς τὸ μὴ κριθῆναι. (fr. 81KA)

Somewhere in *Archilochoi*, and apparently in *Thraittai*, one Callias was ridiculed by the poet, although it is uncertain whether the scholiast meant the elder Callias, the wealthiest man in Athens and friend of Cimon,³³ or his dissolute grandson of the same name, who was frequently mocked by Aristophanes.³⁴ A precise identification,³⁵ however, is of

---

exactly Archilochus' 'Ερασμονίδη . . ." the first colon of Cratinus 11KA has
    x − ∪∪ − ∪ − ∪ −,
  instead of
    x − ∪∪ − ∪∪ − −,
i.e. he changes the second "dactyl" to a "trochee." See West (1982) 97.

31 For other examples of Cratinus' colon division in comedy see West (1982) 97.

32 Luppe (1966) noted that the MS. Δ of the Lucian passage in fact has θρᾶττες, which he then corrects to Θρᾴτταις. Previously it had been assumed that the scholiast was still referring the charge of debt to *Archilochoi*, since MS. V made no mention of a different play.

33 Note the nickname of the elder Callias, λακκόπλουτος = "pit-wealth," (i.e. "the one who has found a buried treasure"). Cf. Plutarch *Aristid.* 5.25; Σ Ar. *Nub.* 64.

34 *Aves* 284-86, *Ran.* 432-34, *Eccl.* 810-11.

35 The effect of Luppe's emendation (see n. 32 above) on the problem of identifying the Callias of the frr., as well as on the dating of *Archilochoi* is considerable, for if Θρᾴτταις is accepted, the charge of debt must be directed against the *younger* Callias on the following grounds: fr. 82KA from *Thraittai* attests to the rhetor Euathlos, who comes in for ridicule as late as Aristophanes *Ach.* 710 (i.e. 425). This suggests a date of c. 430 for *Thraittai* (Geissler, Kassel-Austin). But such a date is clearly too late for an attack on the *elder* Callias, who died c. 446/5. This argument prompts Kassel-Austin to date *Archilochoi* to around the same time (c. 430). This assumes, of course, that the Callias

less concern here than the fact that Cratinus ridiculed a prominent politician in the manner described by the scholiast. Cratinus mocks his Callias in *Thraittai* for his debts, for sleeping with the wife of Phocus, and for trying to bribe his way out of a charge of adultery. The statement that Aristophanes referred to him as "engaging in homosexual lust and dissipated by prostitutes" in his *Horai* (c. 427) attests to the popularity of this "ridicule of Callias" among the comic poets (perhaps begun by Cratinus), and suggests that *Archilochoi* also contained insults of this sort against him. Although the scholiast offers no actual examples of this invective against Callias, the insults were no doubt largely of an obscene nature, in keeping with three of the four charges mentioned above (adultery, homosexuality, prostitution). Insults regarding sexual behavior were, of course, frequent in the iambos. Archilochus, for example, offers a fragment that probably refers to the kind of wanton sexual behavior Callias is charged with here: πολλὰς δὲ τυφλὰς ἐγχέλυς ἐδέξω (fr. 189W): "you have received many blind eels" (where ἐγχέλυς = "penises").[36] Charges of perverse sexuality can be found also in Hipponax fr. 20.2Dg, where Bupalus is called a μητροκοίτης, and fr. 69.7-8Dg, which describes an odd sexual encounter of some sort:

τὸν θεοῖσι<ιν> ἐχθρὸν τοῦτον, ὃς κατευδούσης
τῆς μητρὸς ἐσκύλευε τὸν βρύσσον[37]

Insults concerning homosexuality in particular are also found in the iambos,[38] such as the epithet κίναιδος (Archil. fr. 294W) or the more

---

mentioned in fr. 12KA must also be the younger one. Before Luppe's emendation, scholars assumed that the scholiast was attributing all of Cratinus' charges against Callias to *Archilochoi*. The early date given to that play on the basis of fr. 1KA (cf. above n. 18) assured that any reference to a Callias in that play must have been to the elder one. Yet the charges of the second half of the scholium, now ascribed to *Thraittai*, seemed more appropriate to the younger Callias. Meineke II.i.24, admitted a problem and stated flatly that the *scholiast* must have confused the two Calliases, since charges of debt and adultery could not have been directed against the Callias whom Cratinus attacked in *Archilochoi*. Bergk (1838) 22 and Tanner (1920) 172-87 attempted to argue that the scholiast's charges of financial disgrace against Callias can in fact be ascribed to the elder Callias, but this approach must stand repudiated by Luppe (1966, 1973).

[36] Cf. Henderson (1975) 20 s.v. ἐγχέλυς. Whether or not this fr. is addressed to a man or a woman is uncertain. It could apply equally to a nymphomaniac or an insatiable male homosexual, but in either case, the sexual humor is essentially the same.

[37] βρύσσος ("sea-urchin;") seems to belong to a group of obscene double-entendres associated with sea animals; cf. Henderson (1975) 142. The details of this fragment are obscure, but it is likely that the speaker is accusing someone of maternal incest.

[38] For words relating to homosexuals in the iambic poets, see Henderson (1975) 22. Cf. also Cratinus fr. 3KA: εὕδοντι δ'αἱρεῖ πρωκτός, which seems to be an altered proverb for the sake of a homosexual joke; (πρωκτός is here substituted for κύρτος =

recherché κατωμόχανε (Hipponax fr. 39.1Dg; glossed by Henderson [1975] 22 as "so debauched that his rear end gapes all the way to his shoulders").

Since the invective against Callias occurred in a play concerned with Archilochian poetry and, quite probably, the iambos in general, it is likely that Cratinus was inspired by specific points of diction associated with iambographic invective. We cannot say exactly how Callias was treated in the play, or what the extent of the attack on him was. But since the play seems to have been concerned with literary theory, in which the virtues of invective were extolled (as in frr. 2, 6KA above), it is possible that the attack on Callias served to demonstrate the utility of this poetic style in comedy.

We may conclude our discussion of *Archilochoi* with a fragment that is sometimes attributed to that play (= fr. adesp. 1325K):

Μητίοχος μὲν γὰρ στρατηγεῖ, Μητίοχος δὲ τὰς ὁδούς,
Μητίοχος δ' ἄρτους ἐποπτᾳ, Μητίοχος δὲ τἄλφιτα,
Μητίοχος δὲ πάντα ποιεῖ, Μητίοχος δ' οἰμώξεται.

These lines are quoted by Plutarch (*Mor.* 811f) with no indication of authorship, but they are clearly an imitation of Archilochus fr. 115W:[39]

νῦν δὲ Λεώφιλος μὲν ἄρχει, Λεωφίλου δ' ἐπικρατεῖν,
Λεωφίλῳ δὲ πάντα κεῖται, Λεώφιλον δ' †ἀκουε< >.

The similarly structured comic repetition of the proper name in both fragments suggests a connection between the two immediately. Plutarch cites the comic verses as an example of the ridicule of πολυπραγμοσύνη and its dangers (Μητίοχος δ' οἰμώξεται) and it seems as if Archilochus accuses his Leophilus of the same thing (πάντα κεῖται). Bergk was the first to attribute the Plutarch quotation to Cratinus, on the grounds that such a clear imitation of Archilochus would be most appropriate for a poet composing in an Archilochian style.[40] Plutarch notes that Metiochus was a (corrupt) "friend of Pericles": ... τῇ δι' ἐκεῖνον, ὡς ἔοικε, δυνάμει χρώμενος ἐπιφθόνως καὶ κατακόρως. Since, as we shall see below, Pericles was one of Cratinus' favorite targets (and since Pericles' associates also had to endure comic attacks),[41] the attribution

---

"lobster trap"). Cf. Kock (ad fr. 4K): "deflexit Cratinus proverbium in hominem impudicum podice quaestum facientem."

[39] On this fragment, quoted originally by Herodian (*De Figuris, Rhet. Gr.* viii.548) as an illustration of polyptoton, cf. Lobel (1928) 116 and West (1974) 130.

[40] See Bergk (1838) 11-12; also Schwarze (1971) 167.

[41] See, for example, Plutarch *Pericles* 13.15, and Schwarze (1971) 165.

of the fragment to Cratinus on these grounds is also quite possible.⁴² At any rate, whoever the author was, it is apparent that he saw in the Archilochian lines an early example of political κωμῳδεῖν ὀνομαστί, and noted the generic similarity between the iambic and the comic ψόγος.

Cratinus' own awareness of the nature of the Archilochian ψόγος is evident from a Hesychian gloss on a phrase from *Nomoi* (= fr. 138KA):

Hesychius: Λυκαμβὶς ἀρχή· ὁ Κρατῖνος ἐν Νόμοις, τὸν πολέμαρχον δηλῶν, πρὸς ὃ<ν> ἀπεγράφοντο τὰς τοῦ ἀπροστασίου δίκας.

Photius: Λυκαμβὶς ἀρχή· τοῦ πολεμάρχου, ψυχρῶς, ἐπεὶ ἐπολέμησεν Ἀρχίλοχος τῷ Λυκάμβει· ἐπὶ δὲ τούτου ἀποστασίου καὶ ἐπικλήρων αἱ δίκαι ὑπήγοντο

Hesychius tells us that Cratinus used the expression "Lycambean magistracy" (Λυκαμβὶς ἀρχή) in attacking a polemarch. The gloss added by Photius, ἐπεὶ ἐπολέμησεν Ἀρχίλοχος τῷ Λυκάμβει, is meant to explain logically (ἐπεί) the fact that Cratinus calls the ἀρχή Lycambean. Photius thus implies that the polemarch is "like a Lycambes," and that Cratinus views this polemarch as Archilochus viewed Lycambes, i.e. as an individual worthy of abuse.⁴³ The gloss shows at least that, whatever Cratinus intended exactly by Λυκαμβὶς ἀρχή, it referred to the poetic feud between Archilochus and Lycambes. The fact that Cratinus is able to use an adjectival form of the name presumes an ability to speak of Archilochian literary elements in the abstract. This adjective, of course,

---

⁴² "Die hämmernde Wucht der Invektive, besonders die ständige Namenswiederholung, ist dem 'iambischen' Vorbild Archilochos entlehnt, dessen hauptsächlicher Bewunderer und Nachahmer unter den attischen Komikern Kratinos gewesen ist." (Schwarze [1971] 167).

⁴³ Kock argues that since Lycambes would have been considered a *private* enemy, Cratinus means to single out a certain magistrate with whom he has a personal quarrel, and Kock suggests that the magistrate might even be the archon who denied a chorus to the poet in fr. 20KA, "... is enim lepidissime dici poterat πολέμαρχος, quia τοῦ πρὸς Κρατῖνον πολέμου ἦρξεν. itaque Cratini verba sunt πολέμαρχος, Λυκαμβὶς ἀρχή." Kock bases this last suggestion on Photius' comment, which implies that the phrase Λυκαμβὶς ἀρχή was used to make a joke (a "bad" one, ψυχρῶς). Photius no doubt saw Hesychius' gloss τοῦ πολεμάρχου, and then attempted to explain: "what would be the connection between a polemarch and a Λυκαμβὶς ἀρχή?" The bad joke he finds is that Λυκαμβὶς ἀρχή becomes equivalent to πολέμου ἀρχή = "office of the feud/ beginning of the feud." It is likely also that Photius' phrase ἐπεὶ ἐπολέμησεν Ἀρχίλοχος τῷ Λυκάμβει is meant to impute to Cratinus a humorous, ad hoc etymology of πολέμαρχος, i.e. ἐ<u>πολέμ</u>ησεν Ἀ<u>ρχίλοχος</u>.

would only be intelligible to an audience that was capable of making a typological connection between the scene before them on the stage and the feud between Archilochus and Lycambes. If, as seems likely, Cratinus meant to imply that his relationship with a magistrate was such as Archilochus had with Lycambes, this would indicate that he conceived of his comic ridicule as an activity similar to the Archilochian ψόγος.

As we mentioned earlier, Cratinus also composed comedies that are usually classified as "mythological burlesque," in which well-known mythological scenes or characters were travestied.[44] Cratinus has left titles such as *Nemesis*, *Dionysalexandros*, and *Odysseis*, which attest to his activity in this area, but no substantial fragments survive which might give us a detailed picture of their contents. The late commentator Platonius, as we noted above, claimed that Cratinus' mythological plays contained no personal abuse (ἐπιτίμησις, cf. Koster I.51-52), and he likens them more to Middle Comedy: τοιοῦτος οὖν ἐστιν ὁ τῆς μέσης κωμῳδίας τύπος, οἷός ἐστιν ὁ Αἰολοσίκων Ἀριστοφάνους καὶ οἱ Ὀδυσσεῖς Κρατίνου (Cratinus p. 192 KA = Koster I.29-31). But as we shall see below, while Cratinus may have attacked fewer contemporaries *by name* in these plays, they nevertheless seem to have admitted as much personal attack as his others.

In 1904 the publication of P.Oxy. 663 gave scholars for the first time some idea of the nature of the mythological burlesque.[45] The papyrus offers a fragment of the hypothesis to Cratinus' *Dionysalexandros*, a play which, as the papyrus tells us, parodies the story of the Judg-

---

[44] Apparently these were quite popular in the fifth century, although no substantial example survives; (see Norwood [1931] 23). Parodies of mythological scenes are well attested for the Syracusan poet Epicharmus, active in the first half of the fifth century. In particular, Odysseus, Heracles and Dionysus seem to have been the favorite objects of parody. See Pickard-Cambridge (1962) 255-76. P.Oxy. 2659 (= fr. 81 Austin) offers a partial alphabetical list of titles which are indicative of Epicharmus' concerns, e.g., Ἀταλάνται, Βούσειρις, Γῆ καὶ Θάλασσα, Διόνυσοι, Ἥβας Γάμος. On the problem of whether Epicharmus' dramatic works were called κωμῳδίαι, see Pickard-Cambridge (1962) 276-77 and Cassio (1985) 39-43. Aristotle implies a stylistic connection between Epicharmus and Crates when he mentions them in the same breath at *Poet*. 1449b7, saying that Crates was the first to "abandon the ἰαμβικὴ ἰδέα." Aristophanes describes Crates at *Equ.* 539 as ἀπὸ κραμβοτάτου στόματος μάττων ἀστειοτάτας ἐπινοίας, which, in its contrast to the description of Cratinus' more acerbic style in the lines immediately preceding (526-36; on which see above pp. 38-40), implies that Crates took a wholly different approach to comedy. Σ 537 claims that Crates had been an actor in Cratinus' plays, and then became a poet in his own right. Whether or not this is true, it does seem to reflect a tradition that Crates represented a reaction to Cratinus' comic style.

[45] For a full bibliography up to 1973 see Austin (1973) 35. See also Körte (1904) 481-98, and Schwarze (1971) 6-24.

ment of Paris. In this version Dionysus, in the costume of Paris, is the judge in the goddesses' beauty contest, and Paris enters the scene only later when Dionysus carries Helen over to Troy (= fr. 38KA):[46]

26 Διονυσ[αλέξανδρος
27 ἢ[
28 Κρατ[είνου[47]
         ].
.........]ζητ( )
.........]παν
4 ......]αυτον μη
.....κ]ρίσιν ὁ Ἑρμ(ῆς)
ἀπέρχ]εται κ(αὶ) οὗτοι
μ(ὲν) πρ(ὸς) τοὺς θεατάς
8 τινα π(ερὶ) ὑῶν ποιή(σεως)
διαλέγονται κ(αὶ)
παραφανέντα τὸν
Διόνυσον ἐπισκώ(πτουσι) (καὶ)
12 χλευάζου(σιν)· ὁ δ(ὲ) πα-
ραγενομένων <
                    > αὐτῶι
παρὰ μ(ὲν) Ἥρα[ς] τυραννίδο(ς)
ἀκινήτου, πα[ρ]ὰ δ' Ἀθηνᾶς
16 εὐτυχί(ας) κ(α)τ(ὰ) πόλεμο(ν), τῆς
δ' Ἀφροδί(της) κάλλιστο(ν) τε κ(αὶ)
ἐπέραστον αὐτὸν ὑπάρ-
χειν, κρίνει ταύτην νικᾶν.

---

[46] On the question of why Dionysus ends up as the judge of the beauty contest instead of Paris, see Schwarze (1971) 8-10. He maintains that the fact that Paris wants to hand over Dionysus (and Helen initially) to the Greeks (33ff.) implies that he had been deceived by the god, and so bears him a personal grudge. Dionysus would therefore not only have been playing the *role* of Paris, but would also have actually assumed his form. Schwarze assigns this change of form (i.e. costume) to the time in which the parabasis was being delivered [τινα π(ερὶ) τῶν ποιη(τῶν) διαλέγονται]. The scene beginning at Aristoph. *Ran.* 498, where Xanthias puts on the costume of Heracles and is called Ἡρακλειοξανθίας (499), may give us some idea of the scene in Cratinus' play where Dionysus becomes Διονυσαλέξανδρος.

[47] The title of the play occurs at the top of col. ii, numbered in Kassel-Austin as lines 26-28. The ἢ may = η´ (the number 'eight') and refer to the play's position in a list (Körte [1922] 1648f suggests that it refers to an alphabetical listing). Luppe (1966) 184-91, following Edmonds (1957) 32, argues that ἢ represents the disjunctive ἢ and introduces an alternative play title, such as Ἰδαῖοι.

20 μ(ε)τ(ὰ) δ(ὲ) ταῦ(τα) πλεύσας εἰς
   Λακεδαίμο(να) (καὶ) τὴν Ἑλένην
   ἐξαγαγὼν ἐπανέρχετ(αι)
   εἰς τὴν Ἴδην. ἀκού(ει) δ(ὲ) με-
24 τ' ὀλίγον τοὺς Ἀχαιοὺς πυρ-
25 πολ]εῖν τὴν χώ(ραν) (καὶ) [ζητεῖν
29 τὸν Ἀλέξαν[δ(ρον). τὴν μ(ὲν) οὖν Ἑλένη(ν)
   εἰς τάλαρον ὡς τά[χιστα
   κρύψας, ἑαυτὸν δ' εἰς κριὸ[ν
32 μ(ε)τ(α)σκευάσας ὑπομένει
   τὸ μέλλον. παραγενό-
   μενος δ' Ἀλέξανδ(ρος) κ(αὶ) φωρά-
   σας ἑκάτερο(ν) ἄγειν ἐπὶ τὰς
36 ναῦς πρ(οσ)τάττει ὡς παραδώσων
   τοῖς Ἀχαιοῖ(ς). ὀκνούσης δ(ὲ) τῆς
   Ἑλένη(ς) ταύτην μ(ὲν) οἰκτείρας
   ὡς γυναῖχ' ἕξων ἐπικατέχ(ει),
40 τὸν δ(ὲ) Διόνυ(σον) ὡς παραδοθη-
   σόμενο(ν) ἀποστέλλει, συν-
   ακολουθ(οῦσι) δ' οἱ σάτυ(ροι) παρακαλοῦν-
   τες τε κ(αὶ) οὐκ ἂν προδώσειν
44 αὐτὸν φάσκοντες. κωμωι-
   δεῖται δ' ἐν τῶι δράματι Περικλῆς μάλα πιθανῶς δι'
   ἐμφάσεως ὡς ἐπαγηοχὼς
48 τοῖς Ἀθηναίοις τὸν πόλεμον

8 πιχωνποιη pap. π(ερὶ) τῶν ποιη(τῶν) Körte   13 lac. ind. Blass *APF* 3(1906)
486   16 ευφυκ¹ pap. εὐψυχί(ας) Kassel-Austin

The concluding statement of the fragment is especially significant: "in the play Pericles is made fun of persuasively through 'innuendo', as having brought the war upon the Athenians." On the basis of this statement, since Dionysus causes the Trojan War by his abduction of Helen, it becomes likely that Pericles (as the cause of war at Athens) was understood for Dionysus, and τὸν πόλεμον of line 48 means the Peloponnesian War. Satire of Pericles, of course, was hardly unusual in Old Comedy, especially when the plots were set in Athens. We may recall, for example, *Acharnenses* 530-40, where he is also blamed for the outbreak of the war. But there Pericles is mentioned by name, whereas it seems that in the *Dionysalexandros* (if we can trust the papyrus commentator) he is only implied. The most obvious question is how much satire was actually intended by the poet and readily discernible by the audience? Norwood (1931) 122, while he acknowledges the existence of some satire in the play, warns that "... in the present state of our knowledge, it is best ... to believe that Cratinus is primarily concerned with a riotous travesty of the legend, and works contemporary satire into the fabric purely as an undertone." After seven decades of scholarship on this issue, however, there is little doubt that the whole play can be construed as a sustained allegorical attack on Pericles. Schwarze's detailed discussion of the papyrus shows how every point of the plot as related by the papyrus could refer to the life and activity of the historical Pericles.[48] Schwarze sets out the allegorical attack on Pericles in eight categories which we may briefly summarize here:

(1) Dionysus in the play surreptitiously obtains the judgeship over the beauty contest. This corresponds to the fact that Pericles assumed such judicial powers as to decide on matters of war and peace (cf. Aristoph. *Ach.* 530; Plutarch *Per.* 16).

(2) The goddesses promise Dionysus a τυραννὶς ἀκίνητος, εὐτυχία κατὰ πόλεμον, κάλλιστόν τε καὶ ἐπέραστον αὐτὸν ὑπάρχειν. These three gifts could all relate to Pericles: the charge that he aimed at tyranny was common among the comic poets (cf. Schwarze [1971] 11 n.13); εὐτυχία is reminiscent of his prayer for good fortune at Thuc. 2.13.2; and the erotic gift refers no doubt in some sense to Pericles' affair with Aspasia.[49]

---

[48] Schwarze (1971) 11-21; see also Luppe (1966a) 182-84.

[49] Cf. Aristoph. *Ach.* 523ff., and Schwarze (1971) 13 n.21. The reading of lines 12-19, which summarize the actual judgment of Paris, has caused great debate. Aphrodite seems to promise to make Dionysus/Paris beautiful (17-19). But according to the traditional myth, Paris already is beautiful and Aphrodite's gift is Helen, the most beautiful of women. Attempts have been made to emend the text so that it conforms with our expectation that Aphrodite grant Paris a beautiful woman, rather than beauty itself (cf. Luppe [1975a] 187-90; Ebert [1978] 177-82; Luppe [1980] 154-58). But it may very well be that the peculiarity of Aphrodite's gift to Paris in the *Dionysalexandros* was intended to highlight the allegory of Pericles. Pericles was hardly thought of as a beautiful man; in fact he was often ridiculed for his oddly shaped head (see below pp. 55-56). L. Koenen has suggested to me that by altering the gift of Aphrodite from a beautiful woman to the gift of beauty itself, Cratinus implied that before Pericles could expect to win Aspasia's (= Helen) favor, his own physique would first have to be transformed.

(3) Dionysus' choice of Aphrodite's gift corresponds to the charge that Pericles was more interested in his sensual pleasures than carrying through his professed military strategies.

(4) The Trojan War begins as a direct result of Helen's abduction from Sparta. Similarly, Aspasia was felt by some to have been a cause of the Peloponnesian War.[50]

(5) The Achaeans devastate the land by fire in the hypothesis (line 24), which may well allude to the initial attack of the Spartans upon Attica.[51]

(6) Dionysus' fear of Paris (l.32) can be compared to Pericles' perceived irresponsibility in handling the war, and his fear of the Demos.[52]

(7) The surrendering of Dionysus by Paris to the Greeks (40-41) has been seen as an allusion to the Spartan demand for the banishment of Pericles (as an inheritor of the curse on the Alcmaeonids).[53]

(8) The fact that Dionysus' rout of satyrs tries to prevent his surrender refers to the behavior of Pericles' followers.[54]

While it is likely that Cratinus inherited the *form* of the mythological burlesque from the Epicharmean tradition, his motives seem to be new. The myths and stories have become vehicles of personal ridicule and the intrinsic humor of a mythological parody is no longer the sole end of the play. Although this type of comedy may have avoided singling out citizens ὀνομαστί, the *Dionysalexandros* nevertheless seems to have relied on the language and tone of the ψόγος for its humor.

This can be seen from the first twelve lines of the hypothesis. These lines describe what was probably a parabatic syzygy (much like Aristoph. *Pax* 779-816 or *Vesp.* 1009-1121) where the chorus leader

---

[50] Cf. Cratinus fr. 259KA; Eupolis frr. 267, 294KA. I cannot see why Schwarze (1971) 16 finds a connection between Helen and Aspasia too abstract for the audience to appreciate.
[51] Cf. Norwood (1931) 112 n.2.
[52] Cf. Thuc. 2.21.3, and Plutarch *Per.* 33.33.
[53] Schwarze (1971) 20 suggests that the reason Helen is *not* handed over rests on the allegorical equation: Paris = Demos (tricked by Dionysus/Pericles); Helen = the war itself. That is, the war should be continued, but without Pericles.
[54] This is especially likely in view of Hermippus fr. 47KA, which refers to Pericles as βασιλεῦ Σατύρων. This fr. comes from *Moirai*, which was produced the same year as *Dionysalexandros*; it is probable that Hermippus got the idea for this epithet from Cratinus' play.

comes forward to address the audience: οὗτοι μ(ὲν) πρὸ(ς) τοὺς θεατάς τινα π(ερὶ) ὑῶν ποιή(σεως) διαλέγονται κ(αὶ) παραφανέντα τὸν Διόνυσον ἐπισκώ(πτουσι) (καὶ) χλευάζου(σιν).[55] Possibly, the address to the audience takes place in an anapaestic parabasis,[56] while the ridicule of Dionysus follows in some sort of lyric section.[57] In our discussion of *Ranae* 374-77 (above p. 25), we noted that ἐπισκώπτω and χλευάζω occur as part of the chorus' introduction to their ritual-based invective. The verb χλευάζω (with its compounds) is much stronger than γελάω. Aristotle associates χλευάζω with a kind of ὕβρις (*Rhet.* 1379a). Plutarch views the verb similarly at *Mor.* 1075f (where he has the collocation περιυβρίζουσι καὶ χλευάζουσιν) and at *Mor.* 632b he distinguishes it from παίζω: διὸ καὶ Κριτόβουλον ὁ Σωκράτης εὐπροσωπότατον ὄντα προκαλούμενος εἰς σύγκρισιν εὐμορφίας ἔπαιζεν, οὐκ ἐχλεύαζεν. At *Mor.* 557b Plutarch has the expression σὺν γέλωτι χλευάζων, showing that χλευάζων by itself has a nuance which might need qualification. χλευάζω, that is, implies that a degree of malice lies behind an insult or joke. It indicates "abuse or insult" which may or may not be "funny," and would not be confused with mere pleasantry or mild joking. In view of this it seems that the scene described by the papyrus with the verb χλευάζω must be one that amounted to more than innocuous joking about Dionysus' costume. We may infer that when the commentator summarized the lyric part of the parabasis with ἐπισκώ(πτουσι) (καὶ) χλευάζου(σιν), he was describing a choral scene that had invective content similar to that choral passage in *Ranae*[58] which had been character-

---

[55] The content of this address is uncertain and depends on how one reads line 8: π(ερὶ) ὑῶν ποιή(σεως) or π(ερὶ) τῶν ποιη(τῶν). The papyrus clearly has ὑῶν, though early editors had difficulty making sense of this. Supposing the line corrupt, they adduced other passages from comedy that discuss poets (e.g., *Equ.* 507-550) and other plot summaries such as Hypoth. Aristoph. *Pax* III Coulon 25ff.: ὁ μὲν χορὸς περὶ τῆς τοῦ ποιητοῦ τέχνης ... πρὸς τοὺς θεατὰς διαλέγεται, in support of the latter reading. Handley (1982) 109-117, suggests that P.Oxy 2806 (= Austin [1973] 76) describes what could be summarized as "the generation of sons." This, in turn, would enable him to ascribe this fr. to *Dionysalexandros*, and to affirm the transmitted reading of line 8 of P.Oxy 663.

[56] According to Handley's argument (summarized in the preceding note), the address to the audience would be an iambo-anapaestic epirrhema (specifically the second, cf. Handley p. 111) within the parabatic syzygy.

[57] That these epirrhematic odes were often ideal places for abusive jesting and invective can be seen from Aristophanic examples, e.g., *Pax* 774-818. Cf. Sifakis (1971) 41 (b1). Schwarze (1971) 11 suggests that Dionysus changes into the form of Paris during the parabasis, and his new costume occasions the jests of the chorus.

[58] The commentator may even have borrowed the phrase directly from the *Ran.* passage to describe the scene in Cratinus' play, although it is attested well enough outside of Aristophanes (cf. Luppe [1966a] 170). Luppe, however, rejects the authenticity of ἐπισκώ(πτουσι) on the grounds that the collocation ἐπισκώπτω and χλευάζω is too

ized by the same expression. Wherever this scene actually occurred in *Dionysalexandros*, it does seem likely that it contained verses colored by the diction of the iambographic ψόγος.[59]

Even before the discovery of the hypothesis to *Dionysalexandros* there were a sufficient number of extant fragments to suggest that Cratinus was concerned with using the mythological burlesque for political attack. *Nemesis*, for example, was known as early as Plutarch to contain overt invective against Pericles (fr. 118KA): Περικλέα τὰ μὲν ἄλλα τὴν ἰδέαν τοῦ σώματος ἄμεμπτον, προμήκη δὲ τὴν κεφαλὴν καὶ ἀσύμμετρον. ὅθεν . . . Κρατῖνος ἐν Νεμέσει· μόλ' ὦ Ζεῦ ξένιε καὶ καραιέ.[60] Plutarch here establishes a connection between Zeus and Pericles with which we are familiar from other comic references. Aristophanes *Acharnenses* 530, for example, has Περικλέης οὐλύμπιος, and Cratinus *Thraittai* fr. 73.1-2KA, referring again to Pericles' misshapen head, has:[61]

---

subtle a nuance for the hypothesis. Yet, even if the commentator was incapable of coming up with such a nuance on his own, it would be possible for him simply to borrow the fixed expression from such passages as Luppe cites. What is important, of course, is that something in the diction of Cratinus' text indicated to the commentator that such an expression was appropriate.

[59] The kind of diction implied by ἐπισκώπτω and χλευάζω is also relevant to the question of the identity of the chorus. Since we know from 42-43 that there is a chorus of satyrs following Dionysus, it seems logical that they form the chorus mentioned at line 6 (οὗτοι). Schmid (1946) 77 n. 8, however, suggests that οὗτοι are not satyrs but shepherds, i.e. a second half-chorus, jeering at the deceptive Dionysus-Paris. Luppe (1966a) 187, while arguing persuasively for two choruses, maintains that οὗτοι could refer to a chorus either of satyrs or shepherds. (See his discussion 185-87 on the frequency of double choruses.) The argument for a double chorus here relies heavily on fr. 39KA (from *Dionysalexandros*) ἔνεισι ἐνταυθοῖ μάχαιραι κουρίδες, || αἷς κείρομεν τὰ πρόβατα καὶ τοὺς ποιμένας (first adduced by Körte [1904] 493). Handley (1982) 115, is skeptical of two choruses, though he does not address fr. 39KA. But could the phrase ἐπισκώ(πτουσι) (καὶ) χλευάζου(σιν) describe equally a mockery by *either* half-chorus? If we understand it simply to mean "make fun of" in the most general sense, perhaps so (e.g., Schwarze [1971] 11). Dionysus, then, in his new incarnation as Paris, might be wearing a comical costume which could elicit laughter in a chorus of either satyrs *or* shepherds (as when Heracles first sees Dionysus at *Ran.* 42). But as I have argued above the phrase ἐπισκώ(πτουσι) (καὶ) χλευάζου(σιν) implies that the chorus was engaging in genuine invective against Dionysus rather than in mild banter. Such an activity would hardly seem appropriate to a chorus of satyrs, who are Dionysus' loyal followers (cf. lines 42-43). But if a chorus of *shepherds* — followers of the real Paris — find an imposter in their midst assuming the guise of their master, an invective scene against such an individual would be most fitting.

[60] Kassel-Austin's reading of a problematic fragment (which seems preferable to Kock's [fr. 111]: μόλ' ὦ Ζεῦ ξένιε καὶ μακάριε). The verse is quoted by Plutarch *Per.* 3.5 with the following MS variations: καραιέ Par. 1676, κάριε S, μακάριε Y.

[61] Cf. also Cratinus *Cheirones* frr. 258, 259KA (verses directed against Pericles).

ὁ σχινοκέφαλος Ζεὺς ὁδὶ προσέρχεται
<ὁ> Περικλέης, τᾠδεῖον ἐπὶ τοῦ κρανίου
ἔχων, ἐπειδὴ τοὔστρακον παροίχεται

The plot of *Nemesis* itself, however, as the title suggests, concerns the myth of Nemesis and Zeus, and their offspring, Helen. The more common version of the story is that Zeus impregnated Leda in the form of a swan, from which union Helen arose. Cratinus, however, used a version of the story in which Zeus pursued Nemesis (Leda's mother), who then conceived Helen.[62] In this version, the egg containing Helen (at least according to some accounts) was given over to Leda in Sparta by Hermes to be hatched by her.[63]

As early as Bergk (1838) 130 it was noticed that *Nemesis* probably contained some form of an attack on Pericles, and since then scholars have attempted to reconstruct the nature of this attack. The two major questions that have been posed are (1) If Zeus = Pericles, what does it mean to call Pericles a ξένιος as an insult? (2) If the play is in fact a political allegory, do the other characters, Nemesis, Leda, Helen, correspond to political realities? Since these issues have been well treated elsewhere, we need not discuss them in detail here.[64] Political answers, however, are now generally accepted for both questions. Earlier scholars, for example, beginning with Zündel,[65] believed that the epithet ξένιος as applied to Pericles referred to his attempt to naturalize his illegitimate son by Aspasia (cf. Plutarch *Per.* 37.2). In this case, Zeus = Pericles, Helen = Pericles' son, Nemesis = Aspasia, Leda = mode of acquiring Athenian citizenship. Schwarze, however, has suggested that, since Pericles' son would not technically be a ξένος, but a νόθος, the epithet

---

[62] On Cratinus' sources for this version of the myth, see Luppe (1974) 49-54, (1974a) 193-202, and (1975) 143-44.

[63] Cf. Hyginus *Astron.* ii.8; Ps.-Apollod. 3.10.7; Pausanias 1.33.7. That the Athenians would have known the version of the myth followed by Cratinus seems clear from the context of the Pausanias passage. There, Pausanias is discussing the sanctuary of Nemesis in Rhamnus (in Attica, north of Marathon). As Eratosthenes *Katast.* 25 shows, Rhamnus was a local cult site of Nemesis where, as Pausanias relates, Pheidias carved the myth of Zeus and Nemesis. That Cratinus followed this version of the myth is clear from fr. 115KA, an injunction to *Leda* to take care of the egg, and from frr. 117 and 119KA, which allude to Sparta.

[64] On the first question see, e.g., Godolphin (1931) 423-26. On the allegorical interpretation of the other characters, see Schwarze (1971) 33-40, with detailed bibliography p. 33 n. 67; cf. also Luppe (1974) 56-58, who cautions about over-allegorizing the play.

[65] In Meineke V.i.36.

ξένιος of Zeus-Pericles refers rather to Pericles as the "protector of foreigners" (an allusion to his well-known association with foreigners such as Protagoras, Anaxagoras and Aspasia).[66] To account for the rest of the allegory Schwarze explains that the birth of Helen represents the outbreak of the Peloponnesian war as "caused" by the Megarian decree. Aristophanes, of course, refers to Pericles' Megarian decree as the immediate cause of the war (*Ach.* 517 ff., *Pax* 605 ff.), and Thucydides 1.140 attests to a similar popular sentiment. That the decree was considered to be the main cause of the war, Schwarze argues, shows in a sense that the war is a kind of retribution for the hybris which the decree represents. Thus it is all the more appropriate for *Nemesis* to be the mother of Helen, and this would account for Cratinus' choice of myth. The fact, moreover, that the egg in the myth was carried over to Sparta to be given to Leda corresponds to the fact that the initial debates preceding the war took place there.[67] The war (= Helen) was "hatched," as it were, in Sparta (= Leda).[68]

The details of *Nemesis* will always remain conjectural without further evidence, but the various reconstructions make a good case that, like *Dionysalexandros*, this play too was a thinly veiled attack on Pericles. Although there is no explicit evidence for overt abuse in the few extant fragments, insofar as it was a story intended to be understood as a political attack, it is likely that it also contained the type of diction and tone associated with Cratinus' more directly abusive plays.[69]

---

[66] Schwarze (1971) 35.
[67] Cf. Thuc. 1. 66-67.
[68] "Das politische 'Ei', das in Athen von Perikles im Verein mit 'Nemesis' erzeugt und dann in Sparta ausgebrütet wird, so dass 'Helena', der entscheidende Kriegsgrund, zum Vorschein kommt, ist nach alledem mit grosser Wahrscheinlichkeit eben das megarische Psephisma." Schwarze (1971) 39.
[69] Even Cratinus' *Odysseis*, another mythological burlesque, which Platonius claims contained no personal invective (cf. above n. 15), may have been intended as a ψόγος. The bulk of the surviving fragments show abundant parody of Homer (see in general Norwood's discussion [1931] 129-33), but there is evidence that Hipponax incorporated the ψόγος into his own parody of the *Odyssey*, and it is possible that Cratinus was inspired by this precedent. Hipponax frr. 74-77Dg (= P.Oxy. 2174, first edited by Lobel [1941]) seem to be concerned with Odysseus' *nostos*. Lobel (p. 67) discerns references to "seaweed, after a snack, questions about family, Phaeacians, the lotus, perhaps a dreadful giant, embers, not to mention more problematical indications," namely that fr. 127Dg (Κυψοῦν) can be adduced to restore fr. 77.1Dg ( ]υψου[< Κυψώ a comic syncopation of Καλυψώ). Masson (1962) 143 suggests that the poem had something to do with Bupalus, and follows Diehl in restoring 77.4Dg to ὥσπερ Βού[παλος; cf. also Koenen (1959) 113-14, and (1977) 90. The intrusion of the poet's target into a mythological narrative must indicate either that Bupalus is set fantastically into the situation, or that something in the narrative reminds the poet of Bupalus. In either case, the poem would be a personal attack. Note also the parody of Homer (in dactylic hexameter) in Hipponax fr. 126Dg, which attacks a glutton called Εὐρυμεδοντιάδης, and states a wish that he be treated as a

The testimonia and fragments examined in this chapter suggest that Aristophanes' portrait of his elder contemporary was an accurate one. Whether he was composing comedies that ridiculed individuals directly and ὀνομαστί, or through allegorical plots, Cratinus seems to have adopted the stance of the blame poet similar to that of the iambographic poet. Our discussion of *Archilochoi* has shown that he understood the close relationship between the Archilochian poetic and the inherently satirical impulse of comedy. The virulent language that Cratinus was famous for, and his concern with personal attack, reflect, it seems, a conscious exploitation of this relationship. It is likely, moreover, that in looking to the iambos as a poetic antecedent of comic drama, and by incorporating iambographic elements into his plays, Cratinus succeeded in elevating his genre to a level of literary refinement which it had not attained before. He articulated a literary lineage for Old Comedy, and for the first time helped to define this otherwise eclectic genre for his successors.

φαρμακός. On the possibility that this figure stands for Bupalus, cf. Koenen, (1959) 112-13. Cratinus fr. 152KA, from *Odysseis*, has been interpreted as a poetic statement about the play: νεοχμόν <τι> παρῆχθαι ἄθυρμα: Bergk (1838) 161 suggests that it refers to the poet's "novam . . . et insolentem oblectationem." Perhaps the "new plaything" refers more specifically to the innovation of a sustained political allegory in a mythological plot.

CHAPTER IV
COMIC POET AND ΚΩΜΩΙΔΟΥΜΕΝΟΣ:
Aristophanes' Equites

We have seen in the preceding chapters that Aristotle's term ἰαμ-βικὴ ἰδέα does relate to the historical development of Old Comedy. Aristotle was not concerned to document systematically the interrelationship between comic drama and the iambos, but he correctly recognized that the two genres shared similar poetic goals and conventions. Our examination of other evidence confirms this, and suggests not only that the comic poets of the fifth century felt the element of κωμῳδεῖν ὀνομαστί to be generically related to the iambic ψόγος, but that when they were composing invective, they were conscious of the poetic antecedent in the Ionian iambos, and often deliberately embraced motifs and modes of diction found in that genre. Our study of Cratinus in Chapter III has shown that he was among the first comic poets (and certainly the most important) to exploit this perceived affinity with the iambos. Cratinus seems to have recognized that the activity of the comic poet as public blamer was similar to that of the iambic poets, and that the comic ψόγος could employ literary conventions found in the iambos.

This point has special relevance for our understanding of the comic ψόγος, since it suggests that impersonal, conventional factors influenced the composition of a comic poet's personal attacks. The ψόγος, whether iambic or comic, by nature implies a personal relationship between the poet and a target, an antagonism intended to appear historical. But whereas in the iambos the historical identity of the poets' ἐχθροί is often in doubt, the most prominent targets of the comic poets are indisputably historical figures, and, as a result, the comic ψόγος is often felt to reflect a historical situation. Such an approach, however, ignores the fact that the comic poet crafted his ψόγος in accordance with poetic conventions that existed independently of a particular relationship he may have had with a target. As soon as words are molded into a poetic form the factors of genre and convention must come into play. I would strenuously emphasize here, however, that a poet's meticulous attention to convention in a comic ψόγος need not mean that the work is devoid of meaning, or that the poet is merely making a clever and gratuitous display of literary commonplaces. A poet may attack a target and wish to communicate genuine disapproval of his behavior or of something which that character represents. But precisely because this attack is carefully crafted for specific effect, we must treat it as a poetic creation, even if it offers the pretence of being factual. The relationship between a comic poet and his target must not, in short, be examined without consideration of the fact that the comic ψόγος, as we have discovered, exercised certain literary demands that can be traced to the conventions of the iambos.

Even a glance at the κωμῳδούμενοι[1] of the Old Comic poets ought to make us suspicious about assuming a personal relationship between the poet and his targets, since the same public figures are often ridiculed by several poets. Cratinus, Hermippus and Eupolis, for example, all attacked Pericles at one time or another. Eupolis and Aristophanes ridiculed Socrates, while the politicians Hyperbolus and Cleon were attacked in Aristophanes, Eupolis, Hermippus and Plato Comicus.[2] It is, of course, highly unlikely that these people were attacked because each poet felt personal hostility against them. Nor is there compelling reason to suppose that on every occasion of abuse, the poet was expressing specific disapproval of his κωμῳδούμενος. Rather, a more reasonable *prima facie* inference that can be made from simply charting the κωμῳδούμενοι we know of seems to be that certain individuals were considered to be conspicuously controversial, risible, or otherwise infamous enough to serve as promising material for κωμῳδεῖν ὀνομαστί. The choice of genre, in other words, preceded the choice of content. The comic poet's particular attack may or may not reflect what he "really felt" about them, but such information, I would maintain, cannot be extracted either from the mere existence of a ψόγος, or often even from the content of such passages.[3]

This approach, in its general outline, is not especially novel. Since Gomme's admonitory article, "Aristophanes and Politics" (1962), scholars have recognized the dangers of treating Old Comedy as a collection of historical documents. As I noted at the beginning of this study, however, an exception has usually been made for the portrait of Cleon in Aristophanes, particularly in the *Equites*, which has often been

---

[1] This term, like κωμῳδεῖν ὀνομαστί, is also a legacy of Hellenistic scholarship. On the Hellenistic study of κωμῳδούμενοι, see Steinhausen (1910).

[2] Schmid (1946) 17 n. 6 illustrates just how much overlap there was among the comic poets in their choice of targets.

[3] We may consider, for example, Aristophanes' "relationship" with Cratinus, as it is portrayed in his plays. While Aristophanes seems to respect his elder colleague (see above pp. 38-40), on several occasions he is the butt of gratuitous abuse: cf. *Ach.* 848-49 (a passing, unexpected insult impugning Cratinus' moral character), and 1171-73 (where Cratinus is, again unexpectedly, introduced at the end of an elaborate curse).

considered an extended personal diatribe against the poet's special enemy.[4] In this chapter I shall argue that the attack on Cleon in *Equites* is different from other Aristophanic attacks only in its intensity, and not in its generic nature, that it too was composed as a conventional ψόγος, and that Aristophanes himself was aware of the conventional, essentially iambic, nature of his treatment of Cleon.

Before turning to *Equites*, however, I wish to make several general points about the nature of Aristophanes' κωμῳδούμενοι. Σ *Nubes* 96 (see also above pp. 11-12), speaking of the relationship between Aristophanes and Socrates offers one example of just how whimsical a comic portrait could be:[5]

> ταῦτα πρότερος Κρατῖνος ἐν Πανόπταις δράματι περὶ Ἵππωνος τοῦ φιλοσόφου κωμῳδῶν αὐτὸν λέγει· ἀφ' οὗ στοχαζόμενοί τινές φασιν, ὅτι μηδεμιᾶς ἔχθρας χάριν Ἀριστοφάνης ἧκεν ἐπὶ τὴν τῶν Νεφελῶν ποίησιν, ὅς γε μήτε †ἴδιον μήτε ἁρμόττον, ἀλλὰ μηδὲ πρὸς ἓν ἔγκλημα ἦλθε Σωκράτους†. δύο γὰρ κατ' αὐτοῦ ταῦτα προθεὶς ἐγκλήματα. τὸ περὶ τοῦ οὐρανοῦ ὡς ἔστι πνιγεύς, καὶ ὡς ἱκανός ἐστι τὸν ἥττω λόγον διδάσκειν καὶ τὸν κρείττονα, τὸ μὲν κοινὸν τῶν φιλοσόφων ἁπάντων ἐπήγαγεν ἔγκλημα, φαίνεται δὲ καὶ ἐπὶ τούτῳ ὁ Ἵππων κωμῳδηθῆναι φθάσας· τὸ δὲ τῶν ἐγκλημάτων οὐδὲ τὸ σύνολον ἐπικοινωνεῖ φιλοσοφίᾳ — οὐ γὰρ τοῦτο ἐπαγγέλλονται οἱ φιλόσοφοι, δεινοὺς ποιήσειν λέγειν — ἴδιον δὲ τὸ τοιοῦτο μᾶλλον <τῆς> ῥητορικῆς· <ὡς> ἐπ' ἀμφοτέροις τὸν φιλόσοφον καθαρεύειν. V <οἳ δ', ὅτι ὁλόκληρον εἰς αὐτὸν συνέταξε δρᾶμα, δι' ἔχθραν νομίζουσιν αὐτὸν πεποιηκέναι οὐκ ὀρθῶς οἴονται. πρῶτον μὲν γὰρ Δίφιλος εἰς Βοίδαν τὸν φιλόσοφον ὁλόκληρον συνέταξε ποίημα, δι' οὗ καὶ εἰς δουλείαν ἐρρυπαίνετο ὁ φιλόσοφος· οὐ διὰ τοῦτο δὲ ἐχθρὸς ἦν· ἔπειτα Εὔπολις, εἰ καὶ δι' ὀλίγων ἐμνήσθη Σωκράτους, μᾶλλον ἢ Ἀριστοφάνης ἐν ὅλαις ταῖς Νεφέλαις αὐτοῦ καθήψατο.> Ald.

Although Aristophanes may very well have known that Socrates had no interest in meteorological and physical speculation, at *Nubes* 94-104 he has Strepsiades lump Socrates in with those who say (among other things) that the sky is a πνιγεύς. According to the scholiast, Cratinus

---

[4] One notable exception to the usual tendency to treat Aristophanes' abuse of Cleon as essentially rooted in historical fact is Heath (1987) 24-28.

[5] I reproduce here the text of Holwerda (1977) 31.

ridiculed the philosopher Hippon[6] for his πνιγεύς-theory in a play earlier than *Nubes* (i.e. in *Panoptai*, 435? BC).[7] The scholiast observes that the πνιγεύς-motif occurs in both Cratinus and Aristophanes and is led to conclude that this was simply a common joke used by comic poets against philosophers, regardless of their real doctrines (τὸ μὲν κοινὸν τῶν φιλοσόφων ἁπάντων ἔγκλημα ἐπήγαγεν). He points out that it was not a tenet of Socrates in particular, and that this was used by some as one argument against assuming that the play implied an animosity between the philosopher and the poet (ἀφ' οὗ στοχαζόμενοί τινές φασιν ὅτι μηδεμιᾶς ἔχθρας χάριν Ἀριστοφάνης ἧκεν ἐπὶ τὴν τῶν Νεφελῶν ποίησιν). The two "charges" brought against Socrates in *Nubes* 95-99 (that the universe is a πνιγεύς, and that one should teach the lesser and stronger arguments), he claims, are not especially applicable to the historical Socrates (τὸ μὲν κοινὸν τῶν φιλοσόφων ἁπάντων ... ἔγκλημα, τὸ δὲ ... οὐδὲ τὸ σύνολον ἐπικοινωνεῖ φιλοσοφίᾳ ... ἴδιον δὲ τὸ τοιοῦτο μᾶλλον ῥητορικῆς). The scholiast then concludes that "they are mistaken who think that Aristophanes composed the whole play (sc. *Nubes*) out of hostility (δι' ἔχθραν) towards Socrates." He urges the reader, it seems, to become sensitive to the fictions that a comic poet created in his comedies. His example of how Cratinus' ridicule of Hippon finds its way into a play of Aristophanes, where it is in turn used against Socrates, shows clearly that the comic poet need not be expected to provide a factual portrait of his adversaries. The poet could freely borrow and interchange details depending on his particular purpose and his own conception of what was humorous.

In the case of *Nubes*, scholars have been willing to allow that many elements of the portrait of Socrates were traditional.[8] But for *Equites*,

---

[6] On Hippon see Bergk (1838) 164-85 and Guthrie (1965) 354-58.
[7] On the date of this play cf. Geissler (1925) 23, Schmid (1946) 80 n. 16.
[8] Cf. Dover (1968) lii ff. For a summary (with bibliography) of the problem of Socrates' portrayal in *Nubes*, cf. Nussbaum (1980) 43-47. According to Nussbaum's argument, however, Aristophanes is an unusually systematic critic of Socratic philosophy. If this were at all clear to the audience, however, it seems somewhat surprising that Plato, in *Apol.* 19b2-c6, does not entertain any connection whatsoever between the Aristophanic Socrates and the real one. Even supposing that Aristophanes was seriously criticizing aspects of Socratic teaching (regardless of whether the audience would comprehend), it seems that the audience remembered only the exaggerations and sensational elements, for which fact Plato does not seem to blame the comic poet. We may note that in describing *Nub.*, Socrates refers to "*a Socrates of sorts* (Σωκράτη τινά) wheeled in ..." (cf. *LSJ* s.v. τις A.II.6). With the indefinite article Plato seems to imply that, although the comic poets frequently concerned themselves with contemporary individuals, their particular *treatment* of them, shaped by the conventions of comedy and the poet's conception of his play, often bore little resemblance to reality. Perhaps he intends here to chastise the Athenian audience for being unaware of this, and for not realizing that the use of *Nub.* as evidence of Socrates' character is a weak and naive argument on Meletus'

the assumption persists that the play portrayed a historical feud between the poet and Cleon.⁹ Several factors have given rise to this assumption. First, Aristophanes, on a number of occasions in the *Acharnenses* (300, 377-82, 502-3, 659) mentions a quarrel with Cleon. In fact, vv. 377-82 and 502-3 seem to imply that Cleon had taken the poet to court the previous year for having denigrated Athens in the presence of foreigners. On the basis of these lines, and with the support of the scholia, it has become generally accepted that Cleon prosecuted Aristophanes after the production of *Babylonii* in 426,[10] and that *Equites* was in part composed in retaliation for this.[11] Later references in Aristophanes, such as *Nubes* 549-50 (ὃς μέγιστον ὄντα Κλέων᾽ ἔπαισ᾽ εἰς τὴν γαστέρα, ‖ κοὐκ ἐτόλμησ᾽ αὖθις ἐπεμπηδῆσ᾽ αὐτῷ κειμένῳ) are seen to reinforce the notion that *Equites* was composed for personal reasons. Then, there is the more subjective argument that *Equites*, as a prolonged attack on Cleon, is so relentless in its violence and abuse that, when considered in the light of the lines cited above, it must bear a significant resemblance to reality.

What sets Cleon apart from other Aristophanic κωμῳδούμενοι is that in the *Acharnenses* passages cited above the poet appears to refer to himself and his trouble with Cleon. But even if we grant that in 377-82[12] Dicaeopolis speaks on behalf of the poet,[13] this need not lead us to as-

---

part.
 ⁹ Note, for example, Schmid (1946) 187: "Der Hass des Aristophanes gegen Kleon . . . tritt nach den 'Babyloniern' auch in den 'Acharnern' hervor, in denen die 'Ritter' geradezu angekündigt werden." Gelzer (1970) col. 1400, speaks of Aristophanes' "Feindschaft gegen Kleon"; Dover (1972) 99 says, "Kleon seems to have been the aggressor in the feud."
 [10] On the details of the alleged prosecution(s), see Gelzer (1970) col. 1399. Gelzer notes (col. 1398) that the remarks of the scholia seem to derive solely from Aristophanes' plays. Lefkowitz (1982) 108-9, also emphasizes the inconsistencies of the evidence, and is suspicious of the details of the trial. But while she implies that these details are fabrications of the *vita*-tradition, she never says whether or not she believes that a trial actually took place.
 [11] E.g., Dover (1972) 100, "In *Acharnians* Aristophanes felt able to express himself frankly and uncompromisingly on the subject of the attempted indictment, and thereafter he set about composing this 'blow in the belly', *Knights*."
 [12]   αὐτός τ᾽ ἐμαυτὸν ὑπὸ Κλέωνος ἅπαθον
       ἐπίσταμαι διὰ τὴν πέρυσι κωμῳδίαν.
       εἰσελκύσας γάρ μ᾽ εἰς τὸ βουλευτήριον
       διέβαλλε καὶ ψευδῆ κατεγλώττιζέ μου
       κἀκυκλοβόρει κἄπλυνεν, ὥστ᾽ ὀλίγου πάνυ
       ἀπωλόμην μολυνοπραγμονούμενος.
 [13] As, for example, de Ste. Croix (1972) 363 argues, who speaks of "Dicaeopolis . . . who, alone of Aristophanes' characters of whom we know anything, is *carefully and explicitly identified by the poet with himself*" (emphasis his). This has been called into question by Lefkowitz (1982) 109.

sume that his comments refer to historical events. It is, in fact, essential for a ψόγος to relate an antagonism between the poet and a target, a fact which may be masked in drama by the presence of actors playing parts. In the iamboi of Archilochus and Hipponax, it is the poet (in the first-person) who usually does the attacking,[14] and although the historicity or fictionality of iambographic targets will probably always remain a matter of dispute, few people would maintain that iambographic narratives are to be understood as literal, historical documents, in spite of their historical pretence. In view of our earlier conclusion that the stance of the blame poet adopted by the comic poets is a literary inheritance from the iambos, it is not surprising that a comic poet, even in the first-person, would develop his own fiction around a particular target. To use lines from Aristophanes' plays as proof of a biographical truth is as tenuous as assuming that Archilochus, for example, must have seduced Neobule's sister (as in the Cologne epode), or that Hipponax underwent sexual therapy at the hands of a Lydian woman (fr. 95Dg), merely because they present themselves as doing such things. It makes more sense to understand Aristophanes' allusions to an indictment by Cleon as one element of a fiction of hostility between them propagated by the poet. Such a fiction would be eminently self-serving and self-congratulatory, since the more trouble the poet claims to have received from Cleon, the more this would reflect the power and effectiveness of his ψόγος.

In order to substantiate these claims for the portrait of Cleon in *Equites*, we must now show how Aristophanes composed his attack on him in terms of a conventional iambographic ψόγος. The fact that the play is so unrelenting and monolithic in its violence makes it an ideal subject for such an examination since its very singularity of intent magnifies the iambic elements found in varying degrees in all the plays.[15]

---

[14] It seems to have also been possible to embed an attack on someone in a third-person narration; cf. Archilochus 122W, which, according to Aristotle (*Rhet.* 1418b28) is a ψόγος that presents a "father speaking about his daughter." (cf. also Archilochus 19W; and Dover (1964) 207-8.

[15] This extreme quality of the play has not, however, endeared it to most critics. Note Norwood (1931) 207-8: "The *Knights* is a bad and stupid play . . . this anthology of verbs meaning 'to kick in the stomach' . . . is astounding after the *Acharnians* . . . [Aristophanes'] suffocating rage against Cleon has caused him to forget that anger, however justified, cannot of itself project a work of art." Others are equally offended, such as Schmid (1946) 231, who speaks of "die über alles Mass gehende Heftigkeit seiner [Aristophanes'] Sprache und die Rücksichtslosigkeit seiner Anwürfe." Norwood's appraisal is, of course, extreme, but nevertheless captures the play's essence. Precisely because the play has the appearance of being nothing more than a vindictive, personal attack, the plot ultimately seems narrow and trivial, while the relentless invective scenes seem to serve little purpose in the end. Even Henderson (1975) 67 says that *Equites* ". . . is essentially a vindictive work that grew out of the standing feud between the poet and the politician."

The opening speech of the First Servant reveals the conflict that will become the central theme of the play:

κακῶς Παφλαγόνα τὸν νεώνητον κακὸν
αὐταῖσι βουλαῖς ἀπολέσειαν οἱ θεοί. (2-3)

The elements of this speech are distinctly iambic, from the comic name Παφλαγών to the wish that the gods destroy him.[16] That the Paphlagonian (i.e. Cleon)[17] is characterized as fond of slander (αὐταῖς διαβολαῖς, 7), moreover, foreshadows the reciprocal invective to follow in the two *agones*. The tone of these opening lines of the prologue, however, is hardly solemn, a fact which becomes even clearer from the abundant jokes and word plays that follow in vv. 10, 21-26, 34).

The description of Demos and the Paphlagonian in 40-79 establishes a mood for the opening of the play which is more exuberant than reflective. The playful diction of the passage, in particular, draws attention to this.[18] We find, for example, the following lines describing, respectively, Demos and the Paphlagonian:

... δεσπότης
ἄγροικος ὀργήν, κυαμοτρώξ, ἀκράχολος,
Δῆμος Πυκνίτης, δύσκολον γερόντιον
ὑπόκωφον. (40-43)

---

[16] Cf. e.g., Hipponax fr. 35Dg "ἀπό σ' ὀλέσειεν Ἄρτεμις." — σὲ δὲ κὠπόλλων." Also, fr. 126Dg where the poet wishes for the destruction of the glutton "Eurymedontiades"; in this fr. the comic-abusive epithets ποντοχάρυβδις and ἐγγαστριμάχαιρα function in the same way as Aristophanes' Παφλαγών. "Paphlagon," of course, is a bona fide adjective describing someone from Paphlagonia, but Aristophanes makes it clear that the name itself was intrinsically humorous; cf. *Equ.* 919, *Pax* 314. Cf. the comic toponym at Hipponax fr. 53Dg.

[17] It is obvious from the various topical allusions in the play that the Paphlagonian represents Cleon. Still, it is curious that his name is avoided (he is mentioned only once at 976, and that has no direct reference to the action of the play). This may be an indirect acknowledgement that the resemblance between the two is not meant to be too precise. Note 230-33 where Aristophanes has the First Servant claim that the Paphlagonian's portrait mask was not even like Cleon, because the prop-artists were "afraid" to make it so.

[18] At 37-39, immediately preceding this passage, the Second Servant asks the audience to signal by their facial expressions ἢν τοῖς ἔπεσι χαίρωσι καὶ τοῖς πράγμασιν. This amounts to a request that the audience pay attention to the fine points of language as well as plot in *Equites*.

ἤκαλλ', ἐθώπευ', ἐκολάκευ', ἐξηπάτα
κοσκυλματίοις ἄκροισι, τοιαυτὶ λέγων, (48-49)

The entire passage functions as a preliminary diatribe against Cleon:

οὗτος τῇ προτέρᾳ νουμηνίᾳ
ἐπρίατο δοῦλον βυρσοδέψην, Παφλαγόνα
πανουργότατον καὶ διαβολώτατόν τινα. (43-45)

and culminates in five lines that display iambographic diction:

ἔχει γὰρ τὸ σκέλος
τὸ μὲν ἐν Πύλῳ, τὸ δ' ἕτερον ἐν τἠκκλησίᾳ.
τοσόνδε δ' αὐτοῦ βῆμα διαβεβηκότος
ὁ πρωκτός ἐστιν αὐτόχρημ' ἐν Χάοσιν,
τὼ χεῖρ' ἐν Αἰτωλοῖς, ὁ νοῦς δ' ἐν Κλωπιδῶν. (75-79)

The first of the four place names mentioned, Pylos, has its basis in a historical event — Cleon's recent victory there — but the other three exist solely for the sake of a pun (compare, e.g., Hipponax frr. 4a-b, 53, 95.15, 78.12Dg [on which, see above, p. 10 n. 5]). Here, as often in the iambos, such topographical puns are either obscene, insulting, or both: ὁ πρωκτός ... ἐν Χάοσιν (i.e. among pathics); τὼ χεῖρ' ἐν Αἰτωλοῖς (a pun on αἰτεῖν); ὁ νοῦς δ' ἐν Κλωπιδῶν (his mind always intent on theft).[19] The passage exists primarily for these clever puns, and the very fact that the Athenian audience was meant to find this amusing suggests that there was more at work in the play than the mere venting of spleen against Cleon. For Aristophanes makes us laugh first at his particular manipulation of a conventional type of joke, and only secondarily at its applicability to Cleon. The fact, moreover, that the poet, in his attack on Cleon, employs literary conceits that are paralleled in the iambos suggests an awareness that he was treating his target as a literary bête-noire.

This is even more apparent in the parodos (242-83) and the first epirrhematic agon (284-460), where the diction is also highly iambic and the actual contest becomes subordinate to the dazzle of the language. The opening lines of the chorus threaten with the direct violence we find in Hipponax, and the particular diction and syntax assure a humorous tone:

---

[19] See van Daele ad loc. in Coulon (1923-30) vol. I, 83 n. 2; Henderson (1975) 211.

παῖε παῖε τὸν πανοῦργον καὶ ταραξιππόστρατον
καὶ τελώνην καὶ φάραγγα καὶ Χάρυβδιν ἁρπαγῆς,
καὶ πανοῦργον καὶ πανοῦργον· πολλάκις γὰρ αὔτ' ἐρῶ·
καὶ γὰρ οὗτος ἦν πανοῦργος πολλάκις τῆς ἡμέρας.
ἀλλὰ παῖε καὶ δίωκε καὶ τάραττε καὶ κύκα
καὶ βδελύττου, καὶ γὰρ ἡμεῖς, κἀπικείμενος βόα·   (247-252)

The epithets ταραξιππόστρατον and Χάρυβδιν ἁρπαγῆς are formed along similar lines as Hipponactean compounds like κατωμόχανος (39Dg), ἀνασεισίφαλλος (151Dg) and ποντοχάρυβδις (126.1Dg), and the fourfold mention of the Paphlagonian as πανοῦργος portrays Cleon's role as akin to Hipponax's φαρμακός (frr. 26-30Dg), i.e. one who must be publicly beaten (παῖε παῖε τὸν πανοῦργον 247, ἀλλὰ παῖε καὶ δίωκε καὶ τάραττε καὶ κύνα 251,[20] :: Hipponax fr. 26Dg, κράδῃσι βάλλεσθαι, fr. 30Dg, ... ἐν δὲ τῷ θύμῳ ‖ φαρμακὸς ἀχθεὶς ἑπτάκις ῥαπισθείη). When the Paphlagonian appeals to the audience for help (257), ὡς ὑπ' ἀνδρῶν τύπτομαι ξυνωμοτῶν, the chorus' retort indicates that Aristophanes is less concerned here with political accuracy than with developing his verbal attack. They begin by claiming self-righteously that it is just that the Paphlagonian be attacked (ἐν δίκῃ γ'), since he consumes state money for his own purposes and abuses public officials. Yet the elaborate fig-metaphor (259-65), used to describe his political control over officials (τοὺς ὑπευθύνους σκοπῶν, 259), turns into a metaphor for homosexual perversion:[21]

ἐν δίκῃ γ', ἐπεὶ τὰ κοινὰ πρὶν λαχεῖν κατεσθίεις,
κἀποσυκάζεις πιέζων τοὺς ὑπευθύνους σκοπῶν,
260   ὅστις αὐτῶν ὠμός ἐστιν ἢ πέπων ἢ μὴ πέπων.
264   καὶ σκοπεῖς γε τῶν πολιτῶν ὅστις ἐστὶν ἀμνοκῶν,
265   πλούσιος καὶ μὴ πονηρὸς καὶ τρέμων τὰ πράγματα.
261   κἄν τιν' αὐτῶν γνῷς ἀπράγμον' ὄντα καὶ κεχηνότα,
262   καταγαγὼν ἐκ Χερρονήσου, διαλαβὼν ἀγκυρίσας,
263   εἶτ' ἀποστρέψας τὸν ὦμον αὐτὸν ἐνεκολήβασας.

Ἀποσυκάζω, of course, is one of several common obscenities involving figs.[22] Here, the verb means at first sight "to squeeze figs" in the sense

---

[20] For the expression ταράττω καὶ κυκάω cf. also Cratinus Iunior fr. 7.3KA, and van Leeuwen (1900) ad 251.
[21] I adopt here Brunck's transposition of 261-63 (followed by Coulon).
[22] Cf. Taillardat (1965) 76 Sec. 113; Henderson (1975) 117-18.

of testing which one the speaker wants. Πιέζων, then, on the surface means the same thing, but also carries with it the obscene connotation "to penetrate sexually."²³ The association of figs with genitalia was no doubt a common colloquial obscenity, but it had already entered poetic diction in the Ionian iambos with such occurrences as Archilochus fr. 222W, ἴνας δὲ μελέων <τῶν μέσων> ἀπέθρισε "she peeled back the fig-leaves (prepuce) of my manhood" (Henderson's translation [p. 21]),²⁴ or the epithet συκοτραγίδης (Hipp. 177 [=167W] = Archil. 250W: "son of Fig-muncher" = "son of Cunnilinctor"[?]).²⁵ Aristophanes here relies on a similar double-entendre. Although the Paphlagonian's political crimes are, to be sure, "serious," any mention of figs would immediately alert the audience to an obscene joke (as the chorus makes clear in 261-63). The chorus' initial complaints, in other words, have been deflated to the level of a mere obscene joke at the Paphlagonian's expense, leaving little doubt that the poet's intention was to elicit admiration for his clever obscenity rather than serious outrage at Cleon in particular. In fact, all political issues vanish for the moment, as the actors turn to an exchange of threats (271-75). When politics resurface at 278-79, the reference again turns into a joke:

ΠΑ: τουτονὶ τὸν ἄνδρ' ἐγὼ 'νδείκνυμι, καὶ φήμ' ἐξάγειν
ταῖσι Πελοποννησίων τριήρεσι ζωμεύματα.²⁶

The agon that immediately follows has been introduced by the chorus several lines before (276-77):

ΧΟ: ἀλλ' ἐὰν μέντοι γε νικᾷς τῇ βοῇ, τήνελλά σοι·
ἢν δ' ἀναιδείᾳ παρέλθῃ σ', ἡμέτερος ὁ πυραμοῦς.

These lines emphasize the nature of the contest for political supremacy between the two antagonists: which one can outdo the other in insult and obscenity? By referring to the victory in this contest as a τήνελλα or a πυραμοῦς, i.e. by using the vocabulary of public competition,²⁷ the

---

²³ Henderson (1975) 176.
²⁴ Cf. Taillardat (1965) 72 s.v. ἡ συκῆ (= πέος ad *Eccles.* 807).
²⁵ συκοτραγίδης is cited by Suetonius, Περὶ Βλασφημίας (Taillardat [1967] 223.61), as an epithet used of "cheap" or "thrifty" old men (where figs represent an inexpensive food, cf. Degani on Hipponax fr. 36.5Dg), but an additional sexual nuance seems inevitable.
²⁶ Neil (1901) 45 translates ζωμεύματα as "manufactured broth-stuffs"; see his note ad 279 on nouns ending in -ευμα.
²⁷ Cf. Neil (1901) ad 277.

chorus underlines the formalized nature of this agon.[28] It is not to be an exchange of ideas, but a contest of shouting and creative invective, as the proagon shows. There (284-303) for sixteen lines the antagonists exchange one-line trochaic dimeters, each time trying to cap the other. For example, we find (at 285-87):

> ΑΛ: τριπλάσιον κεκράξομαί σου.
> ΠΑ: καταβοήσομαι βοῶν σε.
> ΑΛ: κατακεκράξομαί σε κράζων,

or (294-95):

> ΠΑ: διαφορήσω σ', εἴ τι γρύξεις.
> ΑΛ: κοπροφορήσω σ', εἰ λαλήσεις.

After the epirrhema we find the following iambic pnigos with its elaborate (and graphic) threat (375-81):

> καί νὴ Δί' ἐμβαλόντες αὐ-
> τῷ πάτταλον μαγειρικῶς
> εἰς τὸ στόμ', εἶτα δ' ἔνδοθεν
> τὴν γλῶτταν ἐξείραντες αὐ-
> τοῦ σκεψόμεσθ' εὖ κἀνδρικῶς
> κεχηνότος
>   τὸν πρωκτόν, εἰ χαλαζᾷ.

We may compare these verses to a passage from *Lysistrata* which also consists of a measured and formalized contest of abuse, where the chorus of Old Men exchange threats with the chorus of Women (351-86). The following selections are especially noteworthy for their iambic background:

> οὐ περικατᾶξαι τὸ ξύλον τύπτοντ' ἐχρῆν τιν' αὐταῖς; (357)

> — εἰ νὴ Δί' ἤδη τὰς γνάθους τούτων τις ἢ δὶς ἢ τρὶς
> ἔκοψεν ὥσπερ Βουπάλου, φωνὴν ἂν οὐκ ἂν εἶχον.
> — καὶ μὴν ἰδού· παταξάτω τις. στᾶσ' ἐγὼ παρέξω
> κοὐ μή ποτ' ἄλλη σου κύων τῶν ὄρχεων λάβηται.

---

[28] The formalized agon appears later in Theocritus, e.g., *Idyll* 5.80-137, on which cf. Merkelbach (1956) 97-133.

— εἰ μὴ σιωπήσει, θενών σου 'κκοκκιῶ τὸ γῆρας.
— ἄψαι μόνον Στρατυλλίδος τῷ δακτύλῳ προσελθών.
— τί δ', ἢν σποδῶ τοῖς κονδύλοις; τί μ' ἐργάσει τὸ δεινόν;
— βρύκουσά σου τοὺς πλεύμονας καὶ τἄντερ' ἐξαμήσω. (360-67)

In each scene the pretence is one of hostility, but the outrageousness of the threats (note such word-play as κεκράξομαί σου . . . καταβοήσομαι βοῶν . . . κατακεκράξομαί σε κράζων, 285-87) and the fact that they are essentially part of a game preclude any seriousness of tone. The mention of Hipponax's target Bupalus in *Lysistrata* 361 indicates that Aristophanes was well aware of the literary provenance of this type of passage. Indeed, the Hipponactean fragments affirm a distinct connection in diction and tone with these Aristophanic contests. For threats of physical violence, we may recall Hipponax's fondness for the verb κόπτω (see above, pp. 14-16):

Fr. 8Dg: δοκέων ἐκεῖνον τῇ βακτηρίῃ κόψαι
Fr. 121Dg: λάβετέ μεο ταἰμάτια, κόψω Βουπάλου τὸν ὀφθαλμόν.
Fr. 122Dg: ἀμφιδέξιος γάρ εἰμι κοὐκ ἁμαρτάνω κόπτων.

Elsewhere we find other references to physical violence probably in invective contexts:[29]

Fr. 25Dg: τὴν ῥῖνα καὶ τὴν μύξαν ἐξαράξασα

Fr. 107.10-13Dg: δακ]τύλους μεταστρέψας·
                 ]ος τε καὶ ῥύδην
                 ].ων δ' αὐτὸν ἀσκαρίζοντα
                 ] ν ἐν τῆι γαστρὶ λὰξ ἐνώρουσα

Fr. 107.32Dg: ν]ενυχμένωι πρωκτῶ[ι

Fr. 133Dg: †ἔξ† τίλλοι τις αὐτοῦ τὴν τράμιν †ὑπόργασαι[30]

---

[29] Along with these passages we may consider fr. 73.4-5W (= 132Dg), which, though corrupt as it stands, probably did refer to a speaker's teeth rattled by a violent blow: ₍οἱ δέ μεο ὀδόντες ‖ ἐν ταῖς γ₍νάθοισι πάντες <ἐκ>κεκινέαται. Degani obelizes the entire line, and will not allow it to stand, with West, as vv. 4-5 of fr. 73 (= P.Oxy. 2174 fr. 4); cf. Bond (1975) 179, and Degani ad fr. 132, p.142. I believe that the fr. refers to the result of fisticuffs rather than to the clattering of the teeth from fear (as Masson [1962] 143).

[30] On τράμις, see above pp. 25-26.

Comic Poet and Κωμῳδούμενος

The extended iambographic invective found in the Strasbourg Epode (= Hipponax fr. 194Dg) also provides a literary background for the elaborate curses found in the Aristophanic passages. The authorship of the Strasbourg epode is in dispute, and arguments have been adduced to ascribe it to Archilochus as well as Hipponax.[31] I favor Hipponactean authorship, and in the following discussion I shall refer to Hipponax as its author, although for our purposes the question is less important than the fact that the epode belongs to the iambos, and as such informs Aristophanic invective:[32]

```
       . [
           η[
       π . [            ]ν[. . .]. . . .[
4          κύμ[ατι] πλα[ζόμ]ενος·
           κἄν Σαλμυδ[ησσ]ῷ̣ι̣ γυμνὸν εὐφρονέστ̣[ατα
           Θρήϊκες ἀκρό[κ]ομοι
           λάβοιεν — ἔνθ<α πόλλ'> ἀναπλήσει κακὰ
8          δούλιον ἄρτον ἔδων —
           ῥίγει πεπηγότ' αὐτόν· ἐκ δὲ τοῦ χν<ό>ου
           φυκία πόλλ' ἐπιχ<έ>οι,
           κροτέοι δ' ὀδόντας, ὡς [κ]ύ̣ων ἐπὶ στόμα
12         κείμενος ἀκρασίηι
           ἄκρον παρὰ ῥηγμῖνα κυμα[. . . . . . . ·
           ταῦτ' ἐθέλοιμ' ἂν ἰδεῖν,
           ὅς μ' ἠδίκησε, λ[ὰ]ξ δ' ἐφ' ὁρκίοισ' ἔβη,
16         τὸ πρὶν ἑταῖρος [ἐ]ών.
```

This fragment offers a standard paradigm of the ψόγος: an injustice perceived by the poet (ὅς μ' ἠδίκησε),[33] and wishes for exaggerated mis-

---

[31] For bibliography see Degani (1983) 168.
[32] Koenen (1977) 73-93 has argued (elaborating an idea of Gercke [1900] 28) that fr. 196Dg should precede 194Dg, and that the two frr. come from one poem. Koenen argues that the poem begins with a narration about a cloak thief (fr. 194), and that the elaborate curses in fr. 196 are directed against him. The argument is tantalizing and may be right, but I fear we still do not have enough evidence to conjoin the two fragments with any certainty. For objections to Koenen's proposal, cf. Degani (1984) 69-70.
[33] A situation in which one party feels wronged by another is common cause for λοιδορία in Aristophanes. An injustice motivates expressions of either violence or blame at *Vesp.* 1017f, *Nub.* 575f, *Aves* 137f; *Pl.* 456f implies that λοιδορία is an expected consequence of injustice: σὺ δ', ὦ κάκιστ' ἀπολουμένη τί λοιδορεῖ ‖ ἡμῖν προσελθοῦσ' οὐδ' ὁτιοῦν ἀδικουμένη;

fortune in the optative (λάβοιεν ... ἐπέχοι ... κροτέοι). The passages from *Equites* and *Lysistrata* above show an identical structure, with the optatives modulated to future indicative for more acerbity. Fraenkel, however, has adduced a passage from *Acharnenses* with even more striking parallels to the Strasbourg epode:[34]

   Ἀντίμαχον τὸν Ψακάδαος, τὸν ξυγγραφῆ, τὸν μελέων ποιητήν,
1151 ὡς μὲν ἁπλῷ λόγῳ κακῶς ἐξολέσειεν ὁ Ζεύς·
   ὅς γ' ἐμὲ τὸν τλήμονα Λήναια χορηγῶν ἀπέλυσ' ἄδειπνον.
1156   ὃν ἔτ' ἐπίδοιμι τευθίδος
    δεόμενον, ἡ δ' ὠπτημένη
    σίζουσα πάραλος ἐπὶ τραπέζῃ κειμένη
    ὀκέλλοι· κᾆτα μέλλοντος λαβεῖν
    αὐτοῦ κύων ἁρπάσασα φεύγοι. (*Ach*. 1150-60)

Fraenkel found this ode reminiscent of the Strasbourg epode primarily in its tone. It seems likely, however, that Aristophanes was alluding quite directly to the iambographic fragment. The following parallel phrases suggest similar contexts, in which the speaker reveals his malevolent wishes for an individual who has wronged him:

  ταῦτ' ἐθέλοιμ' ἂν ἰδεῖν
  ὅς μ' ἠδίκησε, ... (Hipponax v. 14f)

  ὅς γ' ἐμὲ τὸν τλήμονα Λήναια χορηγῶν ἀπέλυσ' ἄδειπνον.
    ὃν ἔτ' ἐπίδοιμι τεύθιδος ... (*Ach*. 1152-56)

Hipponax wishes for his enemy to be shipwrecked (1-8) and itemizes the sufferings he wills upon him. Aristophanes' wish for Antimachus at 1157-60 echoes remarkably Hipponax' wish at 11-13:

    ... ἡ δ' ὠπτημένη
    σίζουσα πάραλος ἐπὶ τραπέζῃ κειμένη
    ὀκέλλοι· κᾆτα μέλλοντος λαβεῖν
    αὐτοῦ κύων ἁρπάσασα φεύγοι. (*Ach*. 1157)

    ὡς [κ]ύων ἐπὶ στόμα
    κείμενος ἀκρασίῃ
    ἄκρον παρὰ ῥηγμῖνα κυμα[....... · (Hipponax vv. 11-13)

---

[34] Fraenkel (1957) 29 n. 1.

The ludicrous wish in Aristophanes that a sizzling eel "run aground (ὀκέλλοι) along the shore (πάραλος) as it lies on the table (ἐπὶ τραπέζῃ)" makes more sense when seen as a variation on (and perhaps even a parody of) the shipwreck motif in the Strasbourg epode.[35] Similarly, the appearance of a dog in *Acharnenses* 1160, snatching away the eel, seems less gratuitous if we suppose that Aristophanes is humorously recalling Hipponax's ὡς [κ]ύων (11), while changing completely the details for his own purpose.

The significance of this should be clear, for if it is true that Aristophanes had in mind the Strasbourg epode as a background for his ψόγος against Antimachus, then it would attest to his awareness of the affinity between iambic and comic poetic invective. The other passages of iambographic invective adduced above, in any case, show at least that Aristophanic invective derived from a similar impulse to do violence verbally to an ἐχθρός out of a sense of righteous indignation, and they displayed a similar fondness for comic exaggeration in diction and tone. These similarities make it difficult to deny that when a comic poet composed a ψόγος of any sort, he did so in accordance with certain literary conventions that existed prior to the details of his abuse — in short, that the poetic form of the ψόγος would influence its content. When we return, then, to the first agon in *Equites* (284ff.), we may conclude that the elaborately crafted contest of abuse between the Paphlagonian/Cleon and the Sausage-seller owes its particular form at least as much to the traditional background of the iambographic ψόγος as to a consuming desire to attack Cleon. As it happens, the main reason why Cleon can play the role of the traditional ἐχθρός so well in Aristophanes (and the other comic poets) is because his historical personality was ideally suited for it. He was both a controversial politician and an eristic individual, whose very character embodied the ψόγος, in both the active and passive sense.[36]

The hyperbolic invective of the first agon of *Equites* is typical of many other passages of the play, and it would be repetitive to catalogue every instance where a connection can be made with the iambos. Practically every page of dialogue scene in the play and most of the choral passages are replete with threats of violence reminiscent of the Hipponactean examples cited earlier. I cite here only a few striking examples:

---

[35] See also Koenen's discussion of this fragment, (1977) 87-91.
[36] See, for example, Thuc. 4.21, who calls Cleon βιαιότατος. Aristotle in the *Ath. Pol.* (28.3) says of Cleon, καὶ πρῶτος ἐπὶ τοῦ βήματος ἀνέκραγε καὶ ἐλοιδορήσατο καὶ περιζωσάμενος ἐδημηγόρησε. (It is true that this sounds as if it might be based on a reading of *Equites*, though the detail that Cleon spoke "with his cloak tied up around him" is not derived from the play).

παῖ' αὐτὸν ἀνδρικώτατα καὶ
γάστριζε... (453f)

μέμνησό νυν
δάκνειν, διαβάλλειν, τοὺς λόφους κατεσθίειν,
χὤπως τὰ κάλλαι' ἀποφαγὼν ἥξεις πάλιν. (495-97)

ΠΑ: οὔτοι μὰ τὴν Δήμητρ' ἔτ' εἰ μή σ' ἐκφάγω
ἐκ τῆσδε τῆς γῆς, οὐδέποτε βιώσομαι.
ΑΛ: εἰ μὴ 'κφάγῃς; ἐγὼ δέ γ', εἰ μή σ' ἐκπίω,
κἂν ἐκροφήσας αὐτὸς ἐπιδιαρραγῶ. (698-701)

To these we may add the final curse of the antepnigos of the second epirrhematic agon (927-40), where the Sausage-seller wishes that the Paphlagonian choke to death on a boiling plate of squid in his haste to get to the assembly in time to receive a bribe.

Comic epithets of abuse, in the manner of Hipponax' κατωμόχανος (fr. 39.1Dg), find their way into *Equites* as in 309 (βορβοροτάραξι), while names employed solely for the sake of a pun, as in Archilochus' Ἐρασμονίδης (168W) can be found, for example, in 898, ἀνὴρ Κόπρειος, or in Cleon's name in the play, Παφλαγών.

As one would expect, the iambic predilection for scatological and sexual obscenity is also evident in *Equites*, in such lines as 658, κἄγωγ' ὅτε δὴ 'γνων τοῖς βολίτοις ἡττημένος (referring to Cleon as cowdung); 721, χὠ πρωκτός οὑμὸς τουτογὶ σοφίζεται; 878, οὔκουν σε δῆτα ταῦτα δεινόν ἐστι πρωκτοτηρεῖν ‖ παῦσαί τε τοὺς κινουμένους. At 364-65 we find:

ΑΛ: ἐγὼ δὲ κινήσω γέ σου τὸν πρωκτὸν ἀντὶ φύσκης.
ΠΑ: ἐγὼ δέ γ' ἐξέλξω σε τῆς πυγῆς θύραζε κύβδα.

Archilochus uses the word κύβδα in fr. 42W to refer, it seems, to the bending over of a woman performing fellatio:

ὥσπερ αὐλῷ βρῦτον ἢ Θρέϊξ ἀνὴρ
ἢ Φρὺξ ἔμυζε· κύβδα δ' ἦν πονεομένη.[37]

---

[37] On Κυψοῦν (Hipp. fr. 127Dg) and Κ]υψοῦ (Hipp. fr. 77.1Dg; on the restoration of this word, cf. above, p. 57, n. 69), which seem to refer to Calypso, cf. Henderson (1975) 22, 183, and above p. 26, n. 57. The formation probably puns on the obscene connotation of κύπτω.

Another sexually obscene motif with an iambographic heritage, cunnilingus,[38] is exploited for comic effect several times in *Equites*. At 351-52, for example, we find:

τί δαὶ σὺ πίνων τὴν πόλιν πεπόηκας, ὥστε νυνὶ
ὑπὸ σοῦ μονωτάτου κατεγλωττισμένην σιωπᾶν;

The use of καταγλωττίζω here is particularly clever since, while functioning superficially as a "legitimate" verb meaning "to talk down,"[39] at the same time it carries with it obvious sexual overtones.[40]

Likewise, the the description of Ariphrades at 1280-89 and his "invention" of a particularly perverse form of cunnilingus, suggests in its obscenity and implicit abusiveness an iambographic heritage. It is generally assumed that Aristophanes' purpose in bringing on Ariphrades was simply to amuse the audience with an interlude before the exodos.[41] Indeed, since the second parabasis (where the Ariphrades-passage occurs) usually serves this dramatic function,[42] it is not odd that its content here has little bearing on the actual plot of the play. Yet, while the chorus may not advance the plot, it does seem to pause for a moment to reflect on the course of the play and on comedy in general. As such, as we shall see, the mention of Ariphrades takes on more significance than is usually allowed.

The syzygy opens with a Pindaric parody that turns into a comic *praeteritio*:

        τί κάλλιον ἀρχομένοι-
1265 σιν ἢ καταπαυομένοισιν
        ἢ θοᾶν ἵππων ἐλατῆρας ἀείδειν
        μηδὲν εἰς Λυσίστρατον,
        μηδὲ Θούμαντιν τὸν ἀνέστιον αὖ λυ-
        πεῖν ἑκούσῃ καρδίᾳ;
1270 καὶ γὰρ οὗτος, ὦ φίλ' Ἄπολλον, <ἀεὶ>
        πεινῇ, θαλεροῖς δακρύοισιν
        σᾶς ἁπτόμενος φαρέτρας
        Πυθῶνι δίᾳ <μὴ> κακῶς πένεσθαι.

---

[38] Cf. Henderson (1975) 22.
[39] Cf., for example, *Ach*. 380, but "note the surrounding sexual imagery" (Henderson [1975] 182).
[40] Cf. *Nub*. 51, where Strepsiades speaks of his wife, ἡ δὲ ... καταγλωττισμάτων, "(smelling) of ... lascivious kisses."
[41] Cf. Neil (1901) ad 1264.
[42] On the other Aristophanic second parabases, see Sifakis (1971) 41, 46-47.

The chorus, it seems, wants to prepare the way for the elaborate description of Ariphrades in the epirrhema by saying, in effect, that they will not sing of the usual comic targets.[43] They imply that the audience is by now used to hearing such men as Lysistratus and Thumantis abused by Aristophanes, and their recurrence in other plays seems to bear this out. Lysistratus, for example, appears in four other places, always a chronically impoverished busybody (*Ach.* 856-59; *Daet.* fr. 205.2KA; *Vesp.* 787, 1302). Thumantis occurs nowhere else in the extant plays of Aristophanes, but he does appear in Hermippus fr. 36KA, representing the same type of person (a beggar) as in the *Equites* passage. These figures, it seems, functioned as stock characters, appearing as they do only when the poet felt a need to ridicule someone who embodied their particular character traits. The mere mention of Lysistratus, in other words, would remind the audience of all the characteristics of beggary. These lines, therefore, draw attention to the fact that the abuse of such characters is a conventional feature of comic drama. This time, says the chorus, they will spare the audience the usual invective passages about the same old butts, and they will move on to a more exotic one — Ariphrades. The humor, of course, lies in the nature of the *praeteritio*: the passage ridicules *en passant* the very individuals it vowed not to.

Before the chorus moves on to their description of Ariphrades, they offer a kind of apologia in the opening lines of the epirrhema (1274-75):

λοιδορῆσαι τοὺς πονηροὺς οὐδέν ἐστ' ἐπίφθονον,
ἀλλὰ τιμὴ τοῖσι χρηστοῖς, ὅστις εὖ λογίζεται.

The immediate function of these lines is to "defend" the highly obscene description of Ariphrades that follows. The chorus sets up for the audience an opposition between the χρηστοί and the πονηροί, characteristic of blame poetry,[44] and as members of the former group, engage in a λοιδορία against the latter. They proceed to describe the πονηρία of Ariphrades (1280-86):

ἔστιν οὖν ἀδελφὸς αὐτῷ [sc. Arignotus] τοὺς τρόπους οὐ συγγενής,
Ἀριφράδης πονηρός. ἀλλὰ τοῦτο μὲν καὶ βούλεται·
ἐστὶ δ' οὐ μόνον πονηρός, οὐ γὰρ οὐδ' ἂν ἠσθόμην,

---

[43] "An explanation or excuse is needed for leaving former butts ... for men like Ariphrades." (Neil [1901] 166).
[44] On the moral self-righteousness of the iambic and comic poet, see the discussion above pp. 18-24.

οὐδὲ παμπόνηρος, ἀλλὰ καὶ προσεξηύρηκέ τι.
τὴν γὰρ αὑτοῦ γλῶτταν αἰσχραῖς ἡδοναῖς λυμαίνεται,
ἐν κασαυρείοισι λείχων τὴν ἀπόπτυστον δρόσον,
καὶ μολύνων τὴν ὑπήνην καὶ κυκῶν τὰς ἐσχάρας ...

This description serves as an exhibition of what comic λοιδορία can be at its most effective. As the chorus says in 1274 (οὐδέν ἐστ' ἐπίφθονον), this kind of language is an honorable thing in the service of abusing individuals such as Ariphrades. When we remember that Cleon (and, in fact, the Sausage-seller) has been consistently treated throughout *Equites* as a πονηρός (e.g., 329, 685-90), it is easy to see that this whole passage reflects on the λοιδορία against him as well. That is, just as the description of Ariphrades (or of a Lysistratus or Thumantis) is justified by the very conventions of comic λοιδορία, so is the attack on Cleon. If it is an "honorable thing" (τιμή, 1275) to make fun of Ariphrades with the obscene diction of 1284-86, then the abuse of Cleon too is honorable, and the violent and obscene approach of *Equites* remains sanctioned by the same poetic traditions.

That Aristophanes considered his attacks on Cleon to be generically akin to his attacks on less conspicuous targets such as Ariphrades becomes clearer from the second parabasis of *Vespae*, which is remarkably similar in function and import to the second parabasis of *Equites*. It too on the surface "is simply an interlude in which Aristophanes amuses the audience by satirical comments on well-known personalities."[45] Like Lysistratus and Thumantis of the *Equites* passage, Amynias of the *Vespae* ode is also famous for his poverty (1270). As in *Equites*, the object of ridicule in the ensuing epirrhema is once again Ariphrades (*Vespae* 1280-83):[46]

εἶτ' Ἀριφράδην πολύ τι θυμοσοφικώτατον,
ὅντινά ποτ' ὤμοσε μαθόντα παρὰ μηδενὸς
[ἀλλ' ἀπὸ σοφῆς φύσεως αὐτόματον ἐκμαθεῖν]
γλωττοποιεῖν εἰς τὰ πορνεῖ' εἰσιόνθ' ἑκάστοτε.

The recurrence of similar character types (beggars, sexual perverts) in identical dramatic *loci* does seem to indicate that the individuals involved were in fact part of the poet's repertoire of κωμῳδούμενοι, cho-

---

[45] MacDowell (1971) 295.
[46] For this passage of *Vespae*, and for 1284-91 quoted below, I print MacDowell's (1971) text.

sen in accordance with established literary convention. The antepirrhema of *Vespae* leads us to view Cleon in this light too (1284-91):

εἰσί τινες οἵ μ' ἔλεγον ὡς καταδιηλλάγην,
ἡνίκα Κλέων μ' ὑπετάραττεν ἐπικείμενος
καί με κακίσας ἔκνισε, κᾆθ', ὅτ' ἀπεδειρόμην,
οἱ 'κτὸς ἐγέλων μέγα κεκραγότα θεώμενοι,
οὐδὲν ἄρ' ἐμοῦ μέλον, ὅσον δὲ μόνον εἰδέναι
σκωμμάτιον εἴ ποτέ τι θλιβόμενος ἐκβαλῶ.
ταῦτα κατιδὼν ὑπό τι μικρὸν ἐπιθήκισα·
εἶτα νῦν ἐξηπάτησεν ἡ χάραξ τὴν ἄμπελον.

Here the poet seems to be alluding to a quarrel he has been engaged in with Cleon. As it is presented, it seems that Aristophanes was abused by Cleon after his production of *Equites*. He then feigned reconciliation (through an apology?), only to retaliate with renewed onslaughts (1291).[47] But the fact that Cleon is treated in the same context as Ariphrades suggests that he too is being treated as a conventional κωμῳδούμενος. As such, the details of the quarrel between Aristophanes and Cleon can easily be seen as an elaborate fiction, capable of traveling from play to play, gaining new additions and twists, and furnishing the poet with new inspiration. Aristophanes certainly implies as much in 1287-89 where he says that the audience was only interested in whether he, when oppressed by Cleon (θλιβόμενος), would be able to come up with some "sort of little joke" (σκωμμάτιον ... τι). When he complains, therefore, (as at *Vespae* 1285-86) that his plays have caused a violent reaction in Cleon, he is essentially suggesting that his plays have been "successful" in their abuse, i.e. that *Equites*, for example, was so good as a ψόγος that it moved Cleon to attack the poet in return. In maintaining a fiction of animosity between himself and Cleon throughout his career (or at least during Cleon's lifetime), Aristophanes placed an individual σφραγίς on his work.[48] Even if a play were not specifically concerned with this animosity, the poet could always allude to it (as he does, for example, throughout *Vespae*) and thereby call to mind an entire fiction

---

[47] See MacDowell (1971) 299 for a detailed reconstruction of the alleged quarrel, based on the passage in *Vespae*.

[48] Aristophanes, of course, did not have a monopoly on attacking Cleon, though he may have attacked him more vigorously and persistently than his colleagues. In any event, it is irrelevant whether a comic poet's claims to uniqueness or originality are legitimate, since such self-aggrandizing claims had become stock themes. Cf. Sifakis (1971) 39f, 62-68.

existing independently of the particular play. In short, Cleon would have been for Aristophanes what Lycambes was to Archilochus, and Bupalus to Hipponax. While these poets composed invectives against a variety of people, their most detailed fictions were reserved for one in particular, and to a great degree they made their literary reputations on these.

The crucial question that remains is: if so many elements of *Equites* are to be seen now as literary convention, as an "inheritance from the iambos," does the play offer anything more than a clever, if humorous, manipulation of these conventions? In downplaying, for example, any necessary connection between the fictions of the plays and biographical truth about the poet, one might object that we are "explaining away" rather mechanically any substance the play might have to offer. In fact, however, this approach ultimately leads to a more sophisticated reading of the play, since *Equites* gains political significance precisely when the audience can transcend the trivial pretence of a real-life quarrel between Aristophanes and Cleon, and approach the essence of what Cleon stands for — unscrupulous demagoguery. If Aristophanes were concerned primarily with attacking Cleon for purely personal reasons, as is usually alleged, it is unlikely that he would have chosen as Cleon's opponent someone as morally despicable as Cleon himself. It is clearly stated on several occasions (e.g., 329, 685-90), as is often noted, that the reason the Sausage-seller wins out over Cleon is because he "out-Cleonizes" him, outdoes him in πονηρία and crudity. Aristophanes, in other words, would never suggest that the Sausage-seller actually replace Cleon as the leader of the people *on moral grounds*. The formalized scenes of violent altercation between the two seem, therefore, to function not so much as a self-righteous, personalized attack on Cleon, as more generalized satire on contemporary demagoguery. The obvious humor of these passages is too pervasive to allow them to be seen as the result of Aristophanes' personal spleen against Cleon. Regardless of what Aristophanes really felt about Cleon, he would have tailored the jokes and word-play of these scenes first and foremost to the audience's awareness of the ἰαμβική ἰδέα.

The amoebean ode between Demos and the chorus at 1111-50 suggests, in fact, that the invective scenes were even less charged with specific political allusion than the audience might have expected up to that point. This short scene functions as an aside to the audience, attuning them to the poet's intentions in dramatizing the λοιδορία between the Sausage-seller and Cleon. The chorus explains that the Demos is too easily led astray and tricked by demagogues:

> ἀλλ' εὐπαράγωγος εἶ,
> θωπευόμενός τε χαί-
> ρεις κἀξαπατώμενος,
> πρὸς τόν τε λέγοντ' ἀεὶ
> κέχηνας· ὁ νοῦς δέ σου
>   παρὼν ἀποδημεῖ. (1115-20)

Demos' reply is both surprising and revealing. He says here that he has actually been aware the whole time of what these demagogues were up to, but that he prefers to let them flatter, cheat, and steal from the state so that when they are "fattened up," he can strike them down (1125-30):

> αὐτός τε γὰρ ἥδομαι
> βρύλλων τὸ καθ' ἡμέραν,
> κλέπτοντά τε βούλομαι
> τρέφειν ἕνα προστάτην·
> τοῦτον δ', ὅταν ᾖ πλέως,
>   ἄρας ἐπάταξα.

In a similar vein, they say at 1145-50:

> τηρῶ γὰρ ἑκάστοτ' αὐ-
> τοὺς οὐδὲ δοκῶν ὁρᾶν
> κλέπτοντας· ἔπειτ' ἀναγ-
> κάζω πάλιν ἐξεμεῖν
> ἅττ' ἂν κεκλόφωσί μου,
>   κημὸν καταμηλῶν.

As a result of this interlude, when the two rivals vie for the affection of Demos in the scenes immediately following, the audience may look upon the egregious flattery of the Sausage-seller and the Paphlagonian from the point of view of Demos himself. They will know that he sees right through the two antagonists, and that it will make little difference which one he prefers in the end. The emphasis in these scenes is less on who in particular is fitting to lead the demos — both are presented as equally undesirable — and more on the way the demos ought to behave.

Aristophanes, in fact, acknowledges that his characters operate in the service of a larger poetic scheme in the parabasis of *Nubes*. The coryphaeus there takes the opportunity, as he does in other parabases (e.g., *Vespae, Pax*), to reflect on the poet's art. After discussing his avoidance of a variety of vulgar dramatic devices, he states at 545-50:

κἀγὼ μὲν τοιοῦτος ἀνὴρ ὢν ποητὴς οὐ κομῶ,
οὐδ' ὑμᾶς ζητῶ 'ξαπατᾶν δὶς καὶ τρὶς ταὔτ' εἰσάγων,
ἀλλ' ἀεὶ καινὰς ἰδέας εἰσφέρων σοφίζομαι,
οὐδὲν ἀλλήλαισιν ὁμοίας καὶ πάσας δεξιάς·
ὃς μέγιστον ὄντα Κλέων' ἔπαισ' εἰς τὴν γαστέρα
κοὐκ ἐτόλμησ' αὖθις ἐπεμπηδῆσ' αὐτῷ κειμένῳ.

He claims here that, unlike his predecessors and rivals, Aristophanes continually brings on "new 'ideas' " that display originality and cleverness. The precise nuance of ἰδέα is difficult to capture in translation, but, to judge from analogous passages in other plays,[49] it seems to mean here a literary "device" or "conceit." With the clause at 549 (ὃς μέγιστον . . .) Aristophanes offers an example of one such "novelty": the attack on someone as great as Cleon at the height of his power. When he goes on to say that he did not overdo this abuse (κοὐκ ἐτόλμησ' αὖθις ἐπεμπηδῆσ' αὐτῷ κειμένῳ, 550), the implication is that this was an artistic choice. That is, if he continued to attack him, the novelty of doing so would have worn thin, and the audience would have lost interest. Similarly, in the remaining lines of the passage, the abuse of individuals is treated as a poetic device, or pretence. There the coryphaeus complains that other poets have copied Aristophanes' device of attacking Hyperbolus, for example:

οὗτοι δ', ὡς ἅπαξ παρέδωκεν λαβὴν Ὑπέρβολος,
τοῦτον δείλαιον κολετρῶσ' ἀεὶ καὶ τὴν μητέρα. (551-52)

εἶθ' Ἕρμιππος αὖθις ἐποίησεν εἰς Ὑπέρβολον,
ἄλλοι τ' ἤδη πάντες ἐρείδουσιν εἰς Ὑπέρβολον,
τὰς εἰκοὺς τῶν ἐγχέλεων τὰς ἐμὰς μιμούμενοι. (557-59)

---

[49] The general meaning behind most of the Aristophanic usages of ἰδέα is "an intellectual formulation" of some sort (cf. *Aves* 993, *Nub.* 289, *Thesmo.* 436; at *Ran.* 382 it means little more than "form," "kind"). At *Vesp.* 1044, however, where Aristophanes complains that the audience failed to understand his play the year before, he says: πέρυσιν καταπροὔδοτε καινοτάτας σπείραντ' αὐτὸν διανοίας ‖ ἃς ὑπὸ τοῦ μὴ γνῶναι καθαρῶς ὑμεῖς ἐποήσατ' ἀναλδεῖς. Here καινὴ διάνοια seems to be identical in meaning to the καινὴ ἰδέα of *Nub.* 547. Other passages in Aristophanes show clearly that διάνοια is included as one of the main literary ingredients (along with τέχνη, diction, and humor) of Aristophanic comedy. See Wilamowitz (1948) 249 on the semantic range of ἰδέα in the late fifth century.

In each case the abuse of politicians is considered solely as a poetic vehicle, whether it is used to shape an entire plot, or to inspire an unusual turn of phrase (cf. 559, where Aristophanes claims that one of his metaphors (εἰκόνες) was actually stolen by another comic poet); there is no mention of any personal motivation lying at the root of this abuse. Aristophanes is saying, in essence, that his rivals stole his idea of a ψόγος against well-known politicians, and he thereby reinforces the argument that the abusive posturings of the comic poet were all part of an elaborate contrivance, with specific traditional demands, designed to amuse and enlighten simultaneously.

EPILOGUE

When it comes to the historical development of personal abuse in Old Comedy, it is obvious that the evidence has allowed me to offer only an incomplete picture. Although all may generally agree that Cratinus was a key figure in emphasizing the poetic ψόγος in Old Comedy, the imperfect chronology of his plays and the paucity of fragments make it difficult to plot a literary history with any certainty. Moreover, our basic ignorance of the comic drama of the period immediately preceding Cratinus, from its "official" acceptance at the Dionysia in 486 to the 450's, makes it difficult to evaluate the later testimonia that regard Cratinus as a solitary innovator. Nevertheless, as we have seen, Aristophanes guarantees sufficiently Cratinus' eminence among fifth-century comic poets, and the accounts of his particularly abusive style are corroborated by the fragments themselves. Though we may never know for sure whether or not Cratinus was singlehandedly responsible for the popularity of κωμῳδεῖν ὀνομαστί at Athens during the last two decades of the fifth century, the evidence we have discussed makes it clear that he had a distinct interest in the literary antecedents of this type of comedy. In particular, his exploitation of the generic affinity between comic drama and the Ionian iambos, as I have argued, must have helped to promulgate a "grammar" of abuse, which furnished his colleagues with a discrete body of verbal, dictional and motival choices in the service of their poetic attacks.

It is in fact the comic poet's consciousness of his poetic activity, first evident in Cratinus, that has been the cornerstone of my argument. As I maintained at the beginning of this study, it is not in itself of great significance that the comic poets exploited poetic conventions found in the iambographic poets. Both the iambos and Old Comedy shared the common social function of personal abuse, and we would of course expect that the conventions common to each would overlap. The fact that many obscenities, for example, found in Old Comedy are paralleled in the iambos need indicate nothing more than their shared generic background: both genres engage in the ψόγος, and obscenity is an effective tool for such a purpose. Other evidence, however, as I have shown, indicates that the Athenian poets of Old Comedy from Cratinus on were in fact aware that when they composed a ψόγος against a particular target, they were working in a literary tradition that had its antecedents in the Ionian iambos. This conclusion may still not allow us to claim that every instance in Old Comedy where diction is paralleled in the iambos implies a direct dependence of the one genre upon the other, but its significance for our understanding of the phenomenon of κωμῳδεῖν ὀνομαστί goes beyond the level of verbal parallels. For the comic poet's desire to emulate the famous ψόγοι of the Ionian iambos implies that he found in them a formal "theoretical" background to his own ψόγοι. The notion that the comic poet was actually conscious of the generic affinity between the iambos and comedy, and that he often deliberately incorporated iambographic elements into his plays, has compelled us to reevaluate the poet's pretence of historical animosity against his targets in the light of the force of literary conventions. As we have seen in the case of Aristophanes' portrait of Cleon, a comic poet's attack may or may not have been heartfelt, but the form it finally took on the comic stage was highly stylized.

Literary conventions, of course, above all serve to delineate the very nature of the work in which they appear; they automatically set the work in a literary and cultural context and to a great extent manipulate the audience's expectations. They provide, in short, one way in which an audience can begin to understand what a writer means. The Athenian audience, as they witnessed more and more the pointed ridicule of known individuals on the stage, must have begun to notice that the treatment of κωμῳδούμενοι employed certain literary patterns that we would call conventions and observed specific rules of dramaturgy. Soon enough the audience would come to the theater expecting to see individuals ridiculed according to these conventions and rules. Consequently, the success of a given ψόγος would be judged by the audience more in terms of how it fulfilled their expectations of the genre than how closely it adhered to reality. As I hope to have shown in this study, the comic poet's self-conscious cultivation of a distinctly iambographic stance gave him greater freedom to remove his ψόγοι to a fictional realm, thereby granting his polemics unlimited imaginative scope. The less constrained a poet is to make his characters and their actions consistent with reality during the course of the play, the more forcefully can he impress upon the audience, once their thoughts and emotions have left the comic world, the social and political realities that motivate his satire.

BIBLIOGRAPHY
OF WORKS CITED

Austin (1973) = C. Austin, *Comicorum Graecorum Fragmenta in Papyris Reperta* (Berlin).
Bakhtin (1968) = Bakhtin, *Rabelais and his World* (Cambridge, Mass.).
Bergk (1838) = T. Bergk, *Commentationum de Reliquiis Comoediae Atticae Antiquae* (Leipzig).
Blaydes (1883) = F. Blaydes, *Aristophanis Pax* (Halle).
Blaydes (1892) = ——, *Aristophanis Equites* (Halle).
Bonanno (1972) = M. Bonanno, *Studi su Cratete Comico* (Padua).
Bonanno (1980) = ——, "Nomi e soprannomi archilochei," *MH* 37 65-88.
Bond (1975) = G. W. Bond, review of West (1971) in *CR* 89 n.s. 25 178-81.
Bremmer (1983) = J. Bremmer, "Scapegoat Rituals in Ancient Greece," *HSCP* 87 299-320.
Burnett (1983) = A. P. Burnett, *Three Archaic Poets* (Cambridge Mass.).
Cairns (1972) = F. Cairns, *Generic Composition in Greek and Roman Poetry* (Edinburgh).
Carrière (1979) = J. C. Carrière, *Le carnaval et la politique* (Paris).
Cassio (1981) = A. C. Cassio, "Attico 'volgare' e Ioni in Atene," *Aion* 3 79-93.
Cassio (1985) = ——, "Two Studies on Epicharmus and his Influence," *HSCP* 89 37-51.
Cassio (1985a) = ——, *Commedia e partecipazione: La* Pace *di Aristofane* (Naples).
Chapman (1978) = G. A. H. Chapman, "Aristophanes and History," *Acta Classica* 21.
Coulon (1923-30) = V. Coulon and H. van Daele, *Aristophane*, 5 vols. (Paris).
Cunningham (1971) = I. Cunningham, *The Mimiamboi of Herodas* (Oxford).
de Ste. Croix (1972) = G. E. M. de Ste. Croix, "The Political Outlook of Aristophanes," in *The Origins of the Peloponnesian War* (Ithaca).
Degani (1973) = E. Degani, "Note sulla fortuna di Archiloco e di Ipponatte in epoca ellenistica," *QUCC* 16 (1973) 79-104 [= *Poeti greci giambici ed elegiaci* (Milan 1977) 106-26].

Degani (1975) = ——, "Hippon. fr. 40 Med." in *Scritti in onore di C. Diano* (Bologna) 113-120.
Degani (1982) = ——, *Poesia parodica greca* (Bologna).
Degani (1983) = ——, *Hipponactis Testimonia et Fragmenta* (Stuttgart).
Degani (1984) = ——, *Studi su Ipponatte* (Bari).
Dover (1964) = K. J. Dover, "The Poetry of Archilochus" in *Entretiens Hardt* 10 (Geneva) 183-222.
Dover (1968) = ——, *Aristophanes Clouds* (Oxford).
Dover (1972) = ——, *Aristophanic Comedy* (Berkeley).
Ebert (1978) = J. Ebert, "Das 'Parisurteil' im Dionysalexandros des Kratinos," *Philologus* 122.177-82.
Edmonds (1957) = J.M. Edmonds, *The Fragments of Attic Comedy* vol. I (Leiden).
Else (1957) = G. Else, *Aristotle Poetics: The Argument* (Cambridge, Mass.).
Fluck (1931) = H. Fluck, *Skurrile Riten in griechischen Kulten* (Endingen).
Fraenkel (1957) = E. Fraenkel, *Horace* (Oxford).
Geel (1828) = J. Geel, in *Bibliotheca Critica Nova* vol. IV (Leiden).
Geissler (1925) = P. Geissler, *Chronologie der altattischen Komödie* (Berlin).
Gelzer (1970) = T. Gelzer, "Aristophanes," *RE Suppl.* XII cols. 1392-1569.
Gentili (1981) = B. Gentili, "Lo statuto dell' oralità e il discorso poetico del biasimo e della lode," *Xenia* 1.13-23.
Gentili (1982) = ——, "Archiloco e la funzione politica della poesia del biasimo," *QUCC* 40 n.s. 11.7-28.
Gercke (1900) = A. Gercke, "Zwei neue Fragmente der Epoden des Archilochos," *Wochschr. f. Klass. Phil* 17.28-30.
Gerhard (1913) = G. Gerhard, "Hipponax," *RE* V.2 cols. 1890-1907.
Giangrande (1963) = G. Giangrande, "The Origin of Attic Comedy," *Eranos* 61.1-24.
Godolphin (1931) = F. R. B. Godolphin, "The *Nemesis* of Cratinus," *CP* 26.423-26.
Gomme (1962) = A. W. Gomme, "Aristophanes and Politics," in *More Essays in Greek History and Literature* (Oxford)
Gomme (1962a) = ——, *A Historical Commentary on Thucydides* II (Oxford).
Graf (1974) = F. Graf, *Eleusis und die orphische Dichtung Athens in vorhellenistischer Zeit* (Berlin).
Guthrie (1965) = W. K. C. Guthrie, *A History of Greek Philosophy* II (Cambridge).

Halliwell (1984) = S. Halliwell, "Ancient Interpretations of κωμῳδεῖν ὀνομαστί in Aristophanes," *CQ* 34.i.83-88.
Halliwell (1984a) = ———, "Aristophanic Satire" in *Yearbook of English Studies* 14.6-20.
Handley (1982) = E. W. Handley, "P.OXY 2806: A Fragment of Cratinus," *BICS* 29.109-17.
Hauvette (1905) = A. Hauvette, *Archiloque: Sa vie et ses poésies* (Paris).
Heath (1987) = M. Heath, *Political Comedy in Aristophanes* (Göttingen).
Henderson (1975) = J. Henderson, *The Maculate Muse* (New Haven).
Hendrickson (1925) = G. L. Hendrickson, "Archilochus and the Victims of his Iambics," *AJP* 46.101-27.
Herter (1947) = H. Herter, *Vom dionysischen Tanz zum komischen Spiel: die Anfänge der attischen Komödie* (Iserlohn).
Holwerda (1977) = D. Holwerda, *Scholia Vetera in Nubes* (Groningen) = vol. I.3.1 of *Scholia in Aristophanem* (cf. Koster [1974]).
Householder (1944) = F. Householder, "PAROIDIA," *CP* 39.1-9.
Jung (1929) = F. Jung, *Hipponax Redivivus* (Bonn).
Kaibel (1899) = G. Kaibel, *Comicorum Graecorum Fragmenta* vol 1 (Berlin).
Kassel-Austin (KA) = R. Kassel and C. Austin, *Poetae Comici Graeci* (Berlin [vol. IV] 1983, [vol III.2] 1984, [vol. VI] 1986).
Kleinknecht (1937) = H. Kleinknecht, *Die Gebetsparodie in der Antike* (Stuttgart-Berlin).
Kock (K) = T. Kock, *Comicorum Atticorum Fragmenta* 3 vols. (Leipzig 1880-88).
Koenen (1959) = L. Koenen, "Θεοῖσιν ἐχθρός: Ein einheimischer Gegenkönig in Ägypten," *CE* 34.103-19.
Koenen (1977) = ———, "Horaz, Catull und Hipponax," *ZPE* 26.73-93.
Körte (1904) = A. Körte, "Die Hypothesis zu Kratinos' Dionysalexandros," *Hermes* 39.481-98.
Körte (1922) = ———, "Kratinos," *RE* XI.2 cols. 1647-56.
Koster (1974) = W. J. W. Koster, *Scholia in Aristophanem Pars I, Fasc. 2: in Nubes* (Groningen).
Koster = W. J. W. Koster, *Scholia in Aristophanem IA: Prolegomena de Comoedia* (Groningen 1975).
Lefkowitz (1982) = M. Lefkowitz, *The Lives of the Greek Poets* (Baltimore).
Lasserre (1950) = F. Lasserre, *Les épodes d'Archiloque* (Paris).
Lasserre (1958) = F. Lasserre and A. Bonnard, *Archiloque: Les Fragments* (Paris).
Latte (1929) = K. Latte, "Hipponacteum," *Hermes* 64.385-88 (=*Kleine Schriften* [Munich 1968] 464-67).

Lobel (1928) = E. Lobel, "Questions Without Answers," *CQ* 22.115-16.
Lobel (1941) = ——, in *The Oxyrhynchus Papyri*, XV (London).
Luppe (1966) = W. Luppe, "Zu zwei Kratinos-fragmenten," *Philologus* 110.134-37.
Luppe (1966a) = ——, "Die Hypothesis zu Kratinos' *Dionysalexandros*," *Philologus* 110.169-93.
Luppe (1973) = ——, "Das Aufführungsdatum der 'Archilochoi' des Kratinos," *Philologus* 117.124-27.
Luppe (1974) = ——, "Die *Nemesis* des Kratinos: Mythos und politischer Hintergrund," *Wissenschaftliche Zeitschrift der Universität Halle* 23.49-60.
Luppe (1974a) = ——, "Zeus und Nemesis in den *Kyprien*: Die Verwandlungssage nach Pseudo-Apollodor und Philodem," *Philologus* 118.193-202.
Luppe (1975) = ——, "Nochmals zur Nemesis bei Philodem," *Philologus* 119.143-44.
Luppe (1975a) = ——, review of Austin (1973), *GGA* 227.179-206.
Luppe (1980) = ——, "Nochmals zum 'Paris'-urteil bei Kratinos," *Philologus* 124.154-58.
MacDowell (1971) = D. M. MacDowell, *Aristophanes' Wasps* (Oxford).
Marzullo (1982) = B. Marzullo, "Platon. *Diff. Com.* 14 (*CGF*, p. 6, 73s. Kai.)," *MCr* XV-XVII.205-6.
Masson (1962) = O. Masson, *Les fragments du poète Hipponax* (Paris).
Meineke = A. Meineke, *Fragmenta Comicorum Graecorum* 5 vols. (Berlin 1839-57).
Merkelbach (1956) = R. Merkelbach, "ΒΟΥΚΟΛΙΑΣΤΑΙ (die Wettgesang der Hirten)," *RhM* 99.97-133.
Meuli (1975) = K. Meuli, "Der Ursprung der Fastnacht" in *Gesammelte Schriften* I (Basel) 283-99 [= "Les origines du Carneval," *Annuaire de la Commission Royale Belge de Folklore*, 15 (1967) 63-85].
Miller (1981) = A. Miller, "Pindar, Archilochus and Hieron," *TAPA* 111.135-43.
Nagy (1979) = G. Nagy, *The Best of the Achaeans* (Baltimore).
Neil (1901) = R. A Neil, *The Knights of Aristophanes* (Cambridge).
Norwood (1931) = G. Norwood, *Greek Comedy* (London).
Nussbaum (1980) = M. Nussbaum, "Aristophanes and Socrates on Learning and Practical Wisdom," *YCS* 26.43-97.
Pellizer (1981) = E. Pellizer, "Per una morfologia della poesia giambica arcaica" in *I Canoni Letterari; Storia e Dinamica* (Trieste) 35-48.
Perry (1952) = B. E. Perry, *Aesopica* I (Urbana).
Perry (1965) = ——, *Babrius and Phaedrus* (Cambridge, Mass.).
Pickard-Cambridge (1962) = A. W. Pickard-Cambridge, *Dithyramb, Tragedy and Comedy*[2] (Oxford).

Pickard-Cambridge (1968) = ——, *The Dramatic Festivals of Athens*² (Oxford).
Platnauer (1964) = M. Platnauer, *Aristophanes' Peace* (Oxford).
Pretagostini (1982) = R. Pretagostini, "Arciloco 'salsa di Taso' negli *Archilochoi* di Cratino (fr. 6K)" *QUCC* 40 n.s. 11.43-52.
Radermacher (1954) = L. Radermacher, *Aristophanes' Frösche*² (Vienna).
Rankin (1975) = H.D. Rankin, "ΜΟΙΧΟΣ ΛΑΓΝΟΣ ΚΑΙ ῾ΥΒΡΙΣΤΗΣ: Critias and his Judgement of Archilochus," *GB* 3.323-34.
Reckford (1987) = K. Reckford, *Aristophanes' Old-and-New Comedy* vol. I (Chapel Hill).
Richardson (1974) = N. Richardson, *The Homeric Hymn to Demeter* (Oxford).
Rösler (1976) = W. Rösler, "Die Dichtung des Archilochos und die neu Kölner Epode," *RhM* 119.289-310.
Rösler (1986) = ——, "Michail Bachtin und die Karnivalskultur im antiken Griechenland," *QUCC* n.s. 23.25-44.
Rosen (1984) = R. M. Rosen, "The Ionian at Aristophanes *Peace* 46," *GRBS* 25.389-96.
Rosen (1988) = ——, "Hipponax, Boupalos and the Conventions of the Psogos," *TAPA* 118 [forthcoming].
Rossi (1976) = L. Rossi, "On the Authenticity of the New Archilochus: Asynarteta from the Archaic to the Alexandrian Poets," *Arethusa* 9.2.207-229.
Roux (1972) = J. Roux, *Euripide: Les Bacchantes* (Paris).
Rusten (1977) = J. Rusten "*Wasps* 1360-1369: Philokleon's ΤΩΘΑΣΜΟΣ," *HSCP* 81.157-61.
Schmid (1946) = W. Schmid, *Geschichte der griechischen Literatur* I.4 (Munich).
Schwarze (1971) = J. Schwarze, *Die Beurteilung des Perikles durch die attische Komödie und ihre historische und historiographische Bedeutung* (Munich).
Segal (1961) = C. Segal, "Dionysus and the Unity of the *Frogs*," *HSCP* 65.207-42.
Sharpley (1905) = H. Sharpley, *The Peace of Aristophanes*, (Edinburgh).
Sifakis (1971) = G. M. Sifakis, *Parabasis and Animal Choruses* (London).
Stanford (1963) = W. B. Stanford, *Aristophanes: The Frogs* (London).
Steinhausen (1910) = J. Steinhausen, ΚΩΜΩΙΔΟΥΜΕΝΟΙ (Bonn).
Taillardat (1965) = J. Taillardat, *Les Images d'Aristophane*² (Paris).
Taillardat (1967) = ——, ed., Suetonius, Περὶ βλασφημίας, Περὶ παιδιῶν, *Extraits byzantins* (Paris).
Tanner (1920) = R. H. Tanner, "The ᾿Αρχίλοχοι of Cratinus and Callias ὁ λακκόπλουτος," *TAPA* 51.172-87.

Tarditi (1968) = G. Tarditi, *Archilochus* (Rome).
ten Brink (1851) = B. ten Brink, "Hipponactea" *Philologus* 6.35-80; 215-27.
Ussher (1973) = R. G. Ussher, *Aristophanes Ecclesiazusae* (Oxford).
van Herwerden (1897) = H. van Herwerden, *Aristophanous Eirene* II (Leiden).
van Leeuwen (1900) = J. van Leeuwen, *Aristophanis Equites* (Leiden).
van Leeuwen (1906) = ——, *Aristophanis Pax* (Leiden).
von Blumenthal (1922) = A. von Blumenthal, *Die Schätzung des Archilochus im Altertume* (Stuttgart).
Welcker (1817) = F. T. Welcker, *Hipponactis et Ananii Iambographorum Fragmenta* (Göttingen).
Wendel (1950) = C. Wendel, "Platonius," *RE* XX.2 col. 2544.
West (1971) = M. L. West, *Iambi et Elegi* vol. I (Oxford).
West (1972) = ——, *Iambi et Elegi* vol. II (Oxford).
West (1974) = ——, *Studies in Greek Elegy and Iambus* (Berlin/New York).
West (1982) = ——, *Greek Metre* (Oxford).
West, S. (1988) = S. West, "Archilochus' Message-Stick" *CQ* 38 (i) 42-48.
Whittaker (1935) = M. Whittaker, "The Comic Fragments in their Relation to the Structure of Old Attic Comedy," *CQ* 29.181-91.
Wiechers (1961) = A. Wiechers, *Aesop in Delphi* (Meisenheim am Glan).
Wilamowitz (1900) = U. von Wilamowitz-Möllendorff, *Die Textgeschichte der griechischen Lyriker* (Berlin).
Wilamowitz (1948) = ——, *Platon*[3] II (Berlin).

INDEX LOCORUM

Aelian
  Var. Hist.
    10.13: 13

Alcidamas
  Tarditi Test. 6: 41 n.14

Anonymous *De Comoedia*
  15ff. (Koster) = Cratinus Test.
    19KA: 41
  24 (Koster) = Cratinus Test.
    2a.10KA: 41 n.17

Archilochus
  19W: 64 n.14
  25.2W: 19
  30-47W: 30 n.74
  42.2W: 10 n.5
  42W: 26 n.57, 74
  43.1W: 19
  82.4W: 19
  91W: 20 n.33
  104 Tard. = 126W: 43 n.23
  109W: 20
  115W: 16 n.31, 26, 47
  122W: 64 n.14
  168W: 10 n.5, 26, 44, 74
  172-81W: 31 n.80
  172W: 19, 32
  174W: 32
  185-87W: 31 n.80
  185W: 10 n.5, 26, 32
  185.1-2W: 17-18
  187W: 17-18, 19
  189W: 46
  196a.22-23W = *P. Col.* II.58: 19 n.41
  213W: 20
  222W: 68
  283W: 19
  294W: 46
  324W: 13 n.16
  331W: 10 n.5, 26

Aristophanes
  Acharnenses
    120: 17 n.33
    300: 63
    377-82: 63, 63 n.12
    380: 75 n.39
    502-3: 63
    517ff.: 57
    523ff.: 52 n.49
    530: 52, 55
    530-40: 51
    595-97: 16 n.31, 44 n.27
    655-64: 19 n.40
    659: 63
    710: 45 n.35
    848-49: 60 n.3
    1150-60: 72-73
    1171-73: 60 n.3
  Aves
    137f: 71 n.33
    284-86: 45 n.33
    869: 17 n.33
    904-59: 17 n.32
    970: 31 n.77
    993: 81 n.49
    1009: 14 n.20
    1701: 42 n.19
  Ecclesiazusae
    810-11: 45 n.34
    883: 30 n.73
    1106: 11
  Equites
    2-3: 65
    7: 65
    10: 65
    21-26: 65
    34: 65
    37-39: 65 n.18
    40-79: 65
    196: 31 n.77
    197-201: 17 n.32
    230-33: 65 n.17
    242-83: 66-70

276-77: 68
284-97: 16 n.31
284-303: 69
284-460: 66-70, 73
285-87: 69-70
309: 74
329: 77, 79
351-52: 75
355: 11 nn.7, 9
364-5: 74
375-81: 69
453f: 74
495-97: 74
507-9: 21 n.46
507-550: 54 n.55
520-25: 38
526-28: 27 n.60
526-36: 37-39
531: 38 n.5
537-40: 38
539: 49 n.44
658: 74
685-90: 77, 79
698-701: 74
721: 74
878: 74
898: 74
899: 10 n.5
919: 65 n.16
927-40: 74
976: 65 n.17
1111-50: 79-80
1264-1273: 75
1274-75: 76-77
1280-86: 76-77
1280-89: 75
1375-80: 29 n.70
1402-05: 23
fr. 205.2KA: 76
fr. 655KA: 23
Lysistrata
  351-86: 69
  357: 69
  360f: 14-15
  361-67: 69-70
  1257: 17 n.33
Nubes
  51: 75 n.40
  94-104: 61
  95-99: 62
  192: 43 n.24

289: 81 n.49
545-50: 63, 81
551-2: 81-82
557-9: 81-82
575f: 71 n.33
710: 10 n.5
Pax
  43-48: 28
  99-101: 34 n.87
  127-30.: 29-31, 34
  133f: 31
  149ff.: 34
  151ff.: 34
  157f.: 34
  162-165: 34 n.87
  314: 65 n.16
  603f: 19-20
  605ff.: 57
  648-57: 30 n.75
  700: 38
  702f: 38 n.5
  750f: 37
  774-818: 54 n.57
  779-816: 53
  929-36: 29 n.70
  1089-94: 17 n.32
  1298: 17 n.33
Plutus
  454: 23 n.51
  456f: 71 n.33
Ranae
  42: 55 n. 59
  354-61: 26-28
  357: 40
  372-76: 25
  374-77: 54
  382: 81 n.49
  409-13: 26 n.57
  416-430: 24-25, 28
  432-34: 45 n.34
  439: 26
  498: 50 n.46
  659f: 15-16
  703-5: 20-21
  704: 17 n.33
  706-17: 21 n.47
  730-33: 23
  856-59: 76
  1034: 17 n.32
Thesmophoriazusae
  436: 81 n.49

Vespae
  787: 76
  1009-1121: 53
  1017f: 71 n.33
  1029-37: 18-19
  1044: 81 n.49
  1169: 11
  1259: 32
  1270: 77
  1280-83: 77:
  1284-91: 78
  1302: 76
  1401-5: 33
  1446-48: 33

Aristotle
 Ath. Pol.
  28.3: 73 n.36
 EN
  1128a23: 1
 Poet.
  1448b27: 1
  1448b32: 4
  1449a3: 1
  1449a10: 4 n.16
  1449b4: 41 n.16
  1449b7: 4, 49 n.44
  1449b8: 1
 Pol.
  1336b20: 9 n.3
 Rhet.
  1379a: 54
  1391a2: 11
  1398b11: 13-14
  1418b28: 64 n.14

Athenaeus
  76c: 9 n.3
  461e: 9 n.3, 10 n.6
  505d: 14 n.20
  667d: 9 n.3
  700d: 9 n.3

Callias
  8KA: 29 n.70

Callimachus
  fr. 90Pf.: 24 n.53
  fr. 191.1-4Pf.: 14 n.26

Catullus
  36.5: 4 n.18
  56.1-2: 44 n.25

Comoed. fr. adesp.
  1325K: 16 n.31, 47

Cratinus
  1.5-6KA: 42 n.18
  1KA: 45 n.35
  2KA: 43, 47
  3KA: 46 n.38
  6KA: 42-43, 47
  11KA: 44
  12KA: 45, 45 n.35
  20KA: 48 n.43
  38KA = *P. Oxy.* 663: 50-51
  39KA: 55 n.59
  73.1-2KA: 56
  82KA: 45 n.34
  115KA: 56 n.63
  117KA: 56 n.63
  118KA: 55
  119KA: 56 n.63
  138KA: 48
  152KA: 57 n.69
  198KA: 39
  211KA: 20
  258KA: 55 n.61
  259KA: 14 n.20, 53 n.50, 55 n.61
  360KA: 44 with n.29

Cratinus Iunior
  7.3KA: 67 n.20

Critias
  DK 88 B44: 13

Dio Chrysostom
 Orat.
  33.9-11: 18 n.38

Diogenes Laertius
 Proem.
  12: 43

Diphilus
  fr.2 Bergk = Scholia Aristoph.
   Nub. 96: 11-12

Epicharmus
   81 Austin = *P. Oxy.* 2659: 49 n.43

Eratosthenes
Katast.
   25: 56 n.63

Eupolis
   132KA: 23-4
   267KA: 53 n.50
   294KA: 53 n.50
   392.1-2KA: 20

Euripides
Bacchae
   68-70: 27 n.59
   fr. 858 Nauck: 17 n.35

Hephaestion
Enchir.
   5: 16 n.30
   15.1ff.: 44
   15.8: 44 n.30

Heraclides Ponticus [ap. Athen. 625c]:
   16 n.30

Heraclitus
   DK 22 B42: 12 n.14

Hermippus
   2W: 9 n.3
   4W: 9 n.3, 10, 10 n.6
   5W: 10-11
   7W: 9 n.3
   8W: 9 n.3
   36KA: 76
   47KA: 53 n.54

Hermippus Historicus
   fr. 63 Wehrli: 14 n.20

Herodas
Mim.
   8.60: 15 n.29
   8.79: 15 n.29

Herodian
De Figuris
   viii.548: 47 n.39

Herodotus
   5.56: 31 n.77

Hesychius
   s.v. λιπερνής: 20
   s.v. Λυκαμβὶς ἀρχή: 48

Hippocrates
De Diaeta Acutorum
   28: 34 n.88

Hipponax
   4a-b: 66
   8Dg: 15 n.29, 70
   17Dg: : 24 n.53
   20.2Dg: 46
   24Dg: 26 n.57
   25Dg: 70
   26-30Dg: 67
   26Dg: 22
   27Dg: 22
   28Dg: 22
   29Dg: 21 n.42, 22
   30Dg: 22
   34Dg: 19
   35Dg: 65 n.16
   37Dg: 16 n.31
   39.1Dg: 47, 74
   39Dg: 67
   51.2Dg: 26
   53Dg: 65 n.16, 66
   69.7-8Dg: 46
   69Dg: 30 n.74
   73.4-5W: 15 n.27, 70 n.29
   73Dg: 70 n.29
   74-77Dg = *P. Oxy.* 2174: 57 n.69
   77.1Dg: 74 n.37
   78.12Dg: 10, 66
   92.2Dg: 19
   92.15Dg: 19
   95Dg: 64
   95.3Dg: 19
   95.7-13Dg: 34
   95.10Dg: 10 n.5
   95.15Dg: 66
   107.10ff.Dg: 70
   107.31Dg: 70
   107.32Dg: 19
   107.32Dg: 26
   107.48Dg: 26

107.49Dg: 21
121Dg: 15, 70
122Dg: 15, 70
126.1Dg: 10 n.5, 67
126Dg: 22, 22 n.49, 57 n.69, 65 n.16
127Dg: 10 n.5, 26 n.57, 57 n.69, 74 n.37
129a.1Dg: 26
132Dg: 15 n.27, 70 n.29
133Dg: 19, 25-26, 30 n.74, 70
151Dg: 67
171Dg: 10 n.5
177Dg = Archil. 250W: 10 n.5, 68
194Dg: 71-73
196.9Dg: 10 n.5, 26
196Dg: 71 n.32
203Dg: 21

Homer
Il.
1.474: 44 n.25
16.747: 43 n.24

Od.
11.604: 39 n.19
24.517: 44 n.25

Horace
Carm.
1.16.3,24: 4 n.18
4.2.5-8: 39 n.7
Ep.
6.11-14: 14 n.26
Sat.
1.4.3: 18 n.38

Hyginus
Astron.
ii.8: 56 n.63

Hypothesis Aristophanes *Pax* III
Coulon 25ff.: 54 n.55

IG II/III^2
2.2325 col. I.50 = Cratinus Test. 5KA: 37

Oenomaus
[ap. Euseb. *Praep. Evang.* 5.32-39]: 41 n.15

Ovid
Ibis
467: 24 n.53

P. Oxy.
663: 50-51
2174: 57 n.69
2659: 49 n.43
2806: 54 n.55

Pausanias
1.33.7: 56 n.63

Persius
Sat.
1.123: 39 n.8

Photius
s.v. λιπέρνητες: 20
s.v. Λυκαμβὶς ἀρχή: 48

Pindar
Ol.
9.1ff.: 13 n.16
Pyth.
2.55: 13
2, 76-78: 32 n.82

Plato
Apol.
19b2-c6: 62 n.8
21b3: 31 n.77
Euthyph. 11d: 14 n.20
Ion
531a2: 12
Legg.
935d: 1 n.1
935e4: 9 n.3
Resp.
332d7: 13
363c: 32 n.82
365c: 13
395e7: 1 n.1

Platonius
Diff. Char.
1-8 (Koster) = Cratinus Test. 17KA: 40-41
15 (Koster) = Cratinus Test. 17KA: 41

Diff. Com.
   6-8 (Koster): 18 n.38
   29-31 (Koster) = Cratinus p. 192
     KA: 49
   30, 51 (Koster) = Cratinus p. 192
     KA: 41 n.15.
   51-52 (Koster) = Cratinus p. 192
     KA: 49

Pliny
  NH
   36.11: 14

Plutarch
  Aristid.
   5.25: 45 n.33
  Mor.
   557b: 54
   632b: 54:
   811f: 47
   1075f: 54
  Per.
   3.5: 55 n.60
   13.15: 47 n.41
   16: 52
   24.9: 14 n.20
   33.33: 53 n.52
   37.2: 56
  Praec. ger. reip.
   6: 20 n.43

Ps.-Apollodorus
   3.10.7: 56 n.63

Ps.-Longinus
  De Subl.
   33.5: 39 n.9

Scholia (Aristophanes)
  Nub.
   64: 45 n.33
   96: 11-12, 61
  Ach.
   119: 17 n.35
  Aves
   1150: 9 n.3
  Equ.
   526: 39 n.11
   529: 39 n.10
   531: 38 n.5
   537: 49 n.44

Pl.
   701: 9 n.3
Ranae
   357: 27 n.60
   661: 15 n.30

Scholia (Callimachus)
   fr. 90: 24 n.53

Scholia (Horace)
  Epodes
   6.14: 24 n.53

Scholia (Lucian)
  Iup. Trag.
   48: 45

Scholia (Pindar)
  Ol.
   10.83b: 11

Semos of Delos
   FGH 396 F23: 4 n.16

Sophocles
   fr. 668 Radt: 27 n.60.

Suda
   s.v. κατειλωτισμένος: 11

Suetonius
   Π. Βλασφ. (Taillardat 223.61): 68 n.25

Sulpicia
  Sat.
   6: 24 n.53

Theocritus
  Idyll
   5.80-137: 69 n.28

Thucydides
   1.66-67: 57 n.67
   1.140: 57
   2.13.2: 52
   2.21.3: 53 n.52
   3.92-3: 10 n.6
   4.21: 73 n.36

Tzetzes
  Chil.
   5.728ff: 21
   5.737ff: 24 n.52

INDEX OF SELECTED GREEK WORDS

Ἄβδηρα: 24 n.53
αἰετός: 32
αἴνιγμα: 31 n.77
αἰνίσσομαι: 28, 30, 31, 31 n.77
αἶνος: 17, 31, 31 n.7, 32
Αἰολοσίκων: 49
αἰσχρολογία: 1, 26, 30, 30 n.73
αἰσχρολογέω: 1 n.1
Αἰσχυλίδης: 26
Αἰσχύλος: 41 n.17
Αἰσωπικός: 32
Αἴσωπος: 30, 31, 33
Ἀλέξανδρος: 51
ἅλμη: 42, 43
Ἀλμίων: 42 n.20
ἀναδιφάω: 43, 43 n.24
Ἀνάνιος: 16 n.30
ἀνασεισίφαλλος: 67
ἀναφλάω: 26
Ἀναφλύστιος: 25, 26
ἀνειλωτίζομαι: 10, 11 n.9
Ἀντίμαχος: 72
Ἀπόλλων: 15, 39, 65 n.16, 75
ἀποστάσιος: 48
ἀποσυκάζω: 67
ἀποτίνω: 42, 43, 43 n.23
ἀπότισις: 43
ἀπροστάσιος: 48
Ἀριστοφάνης: 12, 40, 45, 49, 61, 62
Ἀριφράδης: 76, 77
Ἄρτεμις: 65 n.16
Ἀρχέδημος: 24, 25
Ἀρχίλοχοι: 43, 45
Ἀρχίλοχος: 13, 14, 14 n.20, 32 n.82, 39 n.9, 40, 40 n.13, 41, 41 n.17, 48, 48 n.43
ἀσκαρίζω: 70
Ἀταλάνται: 49 n.44
Ἀφροδίτη: 50

Βάθιππος: 44, 44 n.30
βινέω: 26

βλασφημία: 40, 41
βλάσφημος: 14, 41 n.14
Βοίδας: 11, 61
βόλβιτος: 34
βόλιτος: 74
βορβοροτάραξις: 74
βουπάλειος: 14 n.26
Βούπαλος: 15, 15 n.28, 57 n.69, 69, 70
Βούσειρις: 49 n.44
βρύσσος: 46, 46 n.37
βωμολόχος: 26, 27, 27 n.61

γελάω: 54, 78
γέλοιος (γελοῖος): 1 n.1, 32, 44
γέλως: 19, 32, 54
γεφυρισμός: 4 n.5
γλωττοποιέω: 77
Γοργίας: 14 n.20, 42 n.19

δάκνειν: 74
δάκος: 13, 13 n.17
Δελφοί: 33
δέφομαι: 26
Δῆλος: 15
Δημήτηρ: 74
Δῆμος: 65
διαβάλλω: 41, 62 n.12, 74
διαβολή: 65
διαβολία: 32 n.82
διαβολώτατος: 66
διάνοια: 81 n.49
διασυρμός: 41 n.15
διδάσκω: 18, 61
Διονυσαλέξανδρος: 50 n.46
Διόνυσος: 27, 28, 38, 50, 51, 54, 49 n.44
Δίφιλος: 11, 61
δοκησίσοφος: 28, 29
δωδεκάκρουνος: 39

ἐγγαστριμάχαιρα: 22, 65 n.16
ἐγκύπτω: 25, 26 n.57
ἐγχέλυς: 46, 46 n.36

\<ἐκ\>κεκινέαται: 15 n.27, 70 n.29
Ἑλένη: 51
ἔμφασις: 51
ἐπισκώπτω: 25, 50, 54, 54-55 nn.58-59
ἐπιτίμησις: 40, 49
Ἐρασμονίδης: 10 n.5, 26, 44, 44 n.30, 74
Ἑρμῆς: 50
Ἕρμιππος: 9 n.3, 10
Εὔπολις: 12, 61
Εὐρυμεδοντιάδης: 22, 57 n.69
ἔχθος: 13
ἔχθρα: 61, 62
ἐχθρός: 1, 3, 12, 13, 21, 26, 31, 38, 39, 46, 59, 73

Ζεύς: 55, 55 n.60, 56, 72
ζήλωσις: 40, 41

Ἡράκλεια: 10
Ἡρακλειοξανθίας: 50 n.46
Ἡρακλῆς: 18
Ἥρα: 50
Ἡσίοδος: 43

Θάσιος (Θασίαν ἅλμην): 42, 43
θερμόβουλος: 17, 17 n.35
Θησηίς: 11 n.10
Θούμαντις: 75
Θρᾷτται: 45, 45 nn.32-35
θρᾷττες: 45, 45 n.32
Θρέϊξ: 74
Θρήϊκες: 71

ἰαμβίζω: 4
ἰαμβικὴ ἰδέα: 1, 2, 4 n.17, 12 n.11, 37, 38, 49 n.44, 59
ἴαμβος: 1, 9 n.2, 15, 16 n.30
Ἰδαῖοι: 50 n.47

Ἱππόβινος: 25, 26
Ἱππόκινος: 25 n.54
Ἱππόνικος: 45
Ἵππων: 61
Ἱππῶναξ: 15, 15 n.30
Ἰωνικός: 28, 30 n.73

κάθαρμα: 23 n.51
καθαρμός: 24 n.52
κακαγορία: 13
κακηγορέω: 1 n.1

Καλλίας: 25, 45
Καλυψώ: 57 n.69
κάνθαρος: 10 n.5, 28, 31, 33, 34
καραιός: 55, 55 n.60
κάριος: 55 n.60
καρχαρόδους: 18
κασαλβάζω: 10, 11, 11 nn.7, 9
κασαλβάς: 11
κασαυρεῖον: 77
καταγλωττίζω: 63 n.12, 75
καταγλώττισμα: 75 n.40
κατακράζω: 69, 70
κατατιλάω: 27
κατωμόχανος: 47, 67, 74
Κηρυκίδης: 26, 32
Κλεισθένης: 25
Κλέων: 1, 4, 28, 30, 63, 63 n.12
Κλωπίδαι: 66
Κοννᾶς: 38
κόπρος: 34 n.88
κοπροφορέω: 69
κοπρών: 34 n.87
κόπτω: 15, 15 n.29, 70, 69
Κόρινθος: 26
κρανίον: 56
Κράτης: 4 n.7
Κρατῖνος: 26, 27, 38, 39 nn.10-11, 40, 43, 45, 48, 48 n.43, 49, 55, 61
Κριτόβουλος: 54
κύβδα: 10 n.5, 74
κυλικηγορέω: 10
Κυλικρᾶνες: 10
Κύννα: 18, 19
κύπτω: 10 n.5, 26 n.57, 74 n.7
κύσθος: 25, 26
Κυψώ: 74 n.37
κωμῳδέω: 1 n.1, 28, 45, 51, 61; κωμῳδεῖν ὀνομαστί: 1, 6, 26 n.57, 40, 41, 48, 59, 60, 60 n.1, 83, 84; κωμῳδούμενος: 1, 60, 60 n.1, 61, 63, 77, 84
κωμῳδία: 18 n.38, 28, 40, 40 n.12, 41, 49 n.44, 63 n.12
κωμῳδοποιός: 1, 9 n.3

Λακεδαίμων: 51
λακκόπλουτος: 45 n.33
λακωνίζω: 11
Λαμίας: 19
λαύρα: 34, 34 n.87
Λεώφιλος: 26, 47
Λήναια: 72

Index of Selected Greek Words

λιπερνής: 19, 19 n.42, 20
λιπόπολις: 20
λοιδορέω: 2, 40, 41 n.15, 71 n.33, 73 n.36, 76, 77
Λυκάμβης: 32, 48, 48 n.33
Λυκαμβὶς ἀρχή: 48, 48 n.33
Λυσίστρατος: 75

Μελιτεύς: 45
Μητίοχος: 47
μητροκοίτης: 46
μύζω: 74

Νεμέσις: 55
νεοχμός: 58 n.69
νόθος: 56
Νόμοι: 48
νύσσω: 26, 70

ξένιος: 55, 55 n.60, 56, 57
ξυρέω: 17, 18

Ὀδυσσεῖς: 49
Ὀλύμπιος: 55
Ὅμηρος: 43
ὄρχις: 19, 69
ὀφθαλμός: 15, 18, 70

παίζω: 25
παμπόνηρος: 77
Πανδώρη: 26
παννυχίς: 27
Πανόπται: 61
πανοῦργος: 66, 67
πάραλος: 72, 73
παρασύρω: 38, 39 n.9
παραψιδάζω: 34
Πάριοι: 14
Πασιφίλη: 26
Παφλαγών: 65, 65 n.16, 66, 74
πέος: 68 n.24
Περικλῆς: 51, 55, 56
πίθηκος: 17, 18, 32
πικρία: 42 n.0
πικρός: 41, 41 n.15
πνιγεύς: 61, 62
πονηρία: 2, 76
πονηρός: 23, 67, 76, 77
ποντοχάρυβδις: 22, 65 n.16, 67
προθέλυμνος: 39
προστρόπαιος: 23, 24

πρωκτός: 17, 18, 19, 25, 26, 34 n.87, 46 n.38, 66, 69, 70, 74,
πρωκτοτηρέω: 74
πυγή: 17, 18, 19, 74
Πυθών: 15, 75
Πύλος: 11 n.7, 66

ῥεῦμα: 39
ῥέω: 38, 39, 39 n.7
ῥύδην: 70

σάθη: 19
σαλάκων: 11
σαλακωνίζω: 10, 11
Σαλμυδησσός: 71
Σάννος: 26
σάτυρος: 51
Σεβῖνος: 25, 26
σκληρόπεδος: 10 n.4
σκυλεύω: 46
σκυτάλη: 17, 32
σκῶμμα: 27, 40
σκωμμάτιον: 78
σκώπτω: 18 n.38, 39 n.10
σκῶρ: 34 n.88
σοφιστής: 43
σπατίλη: 28, 30, 34 n.88
σπάτος: 34 n.88
σπληνόπεδος: 10
Στρατυλλίς: 70
σῦκον: 39 n.10
συκοπέδιλος: 38, 39
συκοτραγίδης: 68, 68 n.25
συκοφάντης: 39 n.10
σχινοκέφαλος: 56
Σωκράτης: 12, 54, 61, 62 n.8
σωτηρία: 37

ταραξιππόστρατος: 67
Τάρταρος: 43 n.24
ταυροφάγος: 26, 27, 27 n.60
τιλάω: 35 n.88
τίλλω: 25, 26, 70
τράμις: 19, 25, 70, 70 n.30

Ὑπέρβολος: 4

φάλης: 19
φαρμακός: 21, 22, 22 n.49, 23, 24, 24 n.53, 67, 58 n.69
φαρμάσσω: 16 n.31

φιλόσοφος: 11, 29, 61, 62
φλάω: 26
Φλυήσιος: 26
Φρύξ: 74
Φῶκος: 45

Χαρίλαος: 10 n.5, 26, 44
Χάρυβδις: 67
χέζω: 34
Χερρόνησος: 67
χλευάζω: 10, 25, 50, 54, 54 nn.58-59
χορός: 26, 27, 28, 54 n.5
χρηστός: 16 n.31, 76

Ψακάς: 72
ψέγω: 18 n.38
ψογερός: 13
ψόγος: 1, 2, 3, 3 n.9, 5, 7, 9, 12, 13, 14,
    18, 25, 26, 28, 37, 48, 49, 53, 55, 57
    n.69, 59, 60, 61, 64, 64 n.14, 71, 73,
    83, 84

Ὧραι: 45
ὠφέλιμος: 41

GENERAL INDEX

abuse: 1; comic epithets of: 74; iambographic and comic, involving sexual behavior: 46; ritual, in relation to Old Comedy: 28 n.65; traditional aspects of: 82; conventions of: 59

Aesop: 31; in Aristophanes' *Vespae*: 32

ainos: 31; Aesopic tradition: 31; as invective vehicle: 17; as vehicle for abuse: 31-33; eagle and the dung beetle: 31; fox and monkey in Archilochus: 32; in Hipponax: 33; use in iambos: 31

aischrologia (αἰσχρολογία): 26, 30, 30 n.73

Ananius: 15 n.30

Archilochus, in the rhapsodes' repertoire: 12 n.14; and Lycambes: 14, 19, 48; animal fable (ainos) in: 17, 32; didactic pretence in: 18; political exhortation in: 20; puns on proper names in: 26; quoted by Aristophanes: 17, 20; status in antiquity: 12-13

Ariphrades: 76-78

Aristophanes: 15; quarrel with Cleon: 2-3, 19, 63, 78, 79, 84; allusions to lyric poets in: 17 n.32; and Socrates: 2, 61; Archilochus in: 17, 20; awareness of ἰαμβικὴ ἰδέα: 81; claims to originality in comic abuse: 67; connects ritual abuse and comedy: 28 n.65; didactic pretence in: 18-19; *Equites* as conventional ψόγος: 64; gives religious sanction to ψόγος: 28; Hipponax in: 14-15; Homeric allusions in: 17 n.32; parabasis of *Ranae*: 20-21; parodos of *Ranae*: 24-25; *Pax*, Ionian in: 29 n.69; political advice in: 21; "relationship" with Cratinus: 60 n.3

Aristotle: and ἰαμβικὴ ἰδέα: 59; on Archilochus: 13; on the iambos: 1, 4

audience: attitude towards comedy: 62 n.8

begging procession: 4 n.16

Bupalus: 46, 79; as φαρμακός in Hipponax: 21, 22 n.49; in Aristophanes' *Lysistrata*: 70; punning on his name: 26 n.58; see also Hipponax

Callias: ridiculed in Cratinus: 45, 47

Callimachus: and Hipponax: 24 n.53

carnival: and Old Comedy: 5 n.21

choruses, animal: 38 n.6

Cleon: alleged feud with Aristophanes: 2-3, 19; in Aristophanes: 3, 3 n.8, 23, 29, 30, 60, 63-66, 73, 77-79, 84,; portrait in Aristotle: 73 n.36; represented by "Paphlagonian": 65 n.17

comic poet: awareness of iambographic antecedents: 9, 16; didactic pretence of: 19-24, 28; ridicule of philosophers: 62

Crates: 4, 38, 49 n.44

Cratinus: 37-58 (passim); abuse of Pericles: 47, 55; abusive element in: 43; alleged drunkenness of: 38 n.5; Archilochian influence on: 40-44, 48; *Archilochoi*: 42-48; *Archilochoi*, dating of: 42 n.18, 45 n.35; *Dionysalexandros*: 49-55; first victory: 37; importance for development of ἰαμβικὴ ἰδέα: 38; in Aristophanes: 27, 38; introduction of third actor: 41 n.16; invective style of: 39-40; life and career: 37; mythological burlesque in: 49-58; *Nemesis*: 55-58; political allegory in: 52; refined iambographic antecedents: 58; refinement of Old Comedy: 27 n.61; "relationship" with Aristophanes: 60 n.3; ridicule of philosopher Hippon: 62; style characterized by

Aristophanes: 39; *Thraittai*: 45; use of Archilochian meters: 44
Critias: opinion of Archilochus: 13
cults, religious: relation to the iambos and Old Comedy: 4-5; ritual abuse in: 4
cunnilingus: 75

Demeter, cults of: 4
diction: iambographic and comic, shared: 16
Dionysia: 6
Dionysus, cults of: 4
Diphilus (iambographer): 11-12, 16
dung beetle: as ainos: 30; as cipher for Cleon in Aristophanes' *Pax*: 30; in Aesop: 31; in Aristophanes' *Pax*: 28-29; in Hipponax: 33

epithets, abusive: 65 n.16
Equites: Hipponactean diction in: 73; iambographic elements in: 64-82 (passim); moral issues in: 79; (see also under "Aristophanes")
Eupolis: 12, 20, 60
Euripides: 6; parodied in Aristophanes: 17 n.35

fable, animal: see "ainos"
fellatio: 74

Gephyrismos: 25, 28
Gorgias: calls Plato a "new Archilochus": 14 n.20

Hephaestion: on asynarteta in Archilochus and Cratinus: 44
Hermippus (comic poet and iambographer): 9, 10, 11, 12, 16, 60, 76
Hermippus (historian): 14 n.20
Herodas: Hipponax in: 15 n.29
Hipponax: and Bupalus (q.v.): 14-15, 21-22; and Callimachus: 24 n.53; fondness of neologism: 10 n.5; in Aristophanes: 14-15; in Herodas: 15 n.29; obscene diction in: 25; puns on proper names: 26; scatological humor in: 33; status in fifth century: 12-14; violence in: 15
Hippon (philosopher): 62
Horace: on Old Comedy: 18 n.38

Hyperbolus: 60

Iambe: as aitiological figure: 4
iambos: 3, 10; affinities with Old Comedy: 59; αἰσχρολογία in: 30; among Latin writers: 4 n.18; and religious cult: 4; Aristotle on: 1; as a meter: 4; as antecedent of comic ψόγος: 3; as antecedent of Old Comedy: 1; as poetic genre: 3; as poetry of abuse: 3-4; didactic pretence of: 18-19; generic affinity with Old Comedy: 83; historical pretence of narrative in: 64; in the fifth century: 9, 12, 16; obscenity in: 1, 4, 26, 30; personal abuse in: 5; picaresque narrative in: 4; proper names in: 26 n.58 ; in parodos of *Ranae*: 24; ritual origins of: 6, 26; sexual and scatological obscenity in: 19; subjective "I" in: 5; use of ainos in: 31; use of obscenity in: 1, 4, 26, 30
invective: ritual: 4, 25
Ionian: in Aristophanes' *Pax*: 28-35
Ionians: conception of in fifth century: 29 n.70
"Ionian song": 30 n.73

κωμῳδούμενος: 28, 60-61, 77-78, 84

Lycambes: 32, 48-49, 79, 30 n.74, 48 n.43; see also "Archilochus"

Magnes: 38
Megarian decree: 57
mythological burlesque: 49-58; invective diction in: 53; political allegory in: 55

names, proper: 26 n.58
neologism: 10

obscenity: 4-6, 9, 10, 11, 19, 26, 30, 46 n.37, 67-68, 74-75, 77, 83
Old Comedy: affinity with iambos: 6, 83; anthropological approaches to: 5; as didactic genre: 18 n.38, 19 n.40; invective element in: 1, 4-5; jokes against philosophers: 62; literary self-consciousness in: 6; ritual origins of: 4, 6, 28; self-righteous pretence of: 27; social function of: 6

paratragedy: 17 n.32
patronymics: in iambos and Old Comedy: 44
Pericles: ridiculed in Cratinus: 47, 51, 55; comic abuse of: 51, 60
Persius: opinion of Cratinus: 39 n.8
phallic processions, and Old Comedy: 4 n.16
Pindar: Archilochus in: 13
Plato Comicus: 60
Platonius: 40, 41
Pliny: on Hipponax and Bupalus: 14 n. 25
political satire: in the comic parabasis: 21 n.46
psogos (ψόγος): 9, 12; as fiction of hostility created by poet: 64; as poetic genre: 3; conventional aspects of: 5, 59, 73; embedded in a third-person narrative: 64 n.4; implies relationship between poet and target: 59; in Aristophanes: 28; motivated by injustice perceived by poet: 71; pretence of historicity: 60; relates antagonism between poet and target: 64; relationship between iambic and comic: 3
puns: 10, 11, 19, 26, 66, 74

ridicule: (see "abuse")

scapegoat (φαρμακός): in Hipponax: 21-22; in Old Comedy: 22-24
scatology: 74; in Aristophanes: 34; in Hipponax: 33; jokes involving: 29, 30
scatophagy: 30; imputed to Cleon: 31; jokes on: 31 n.76, 34 n.88
Socrates: attacked in Old Comedy: 60; in Aristophanes *Nubes*: 2, 62; relationship with Aristophanes: 61
Strasbourg Epode: 71; and Aristophanes: 73

target (of abuse): 2, 57 n.69; and relationship with poet: 5; *Thraittai*: 45-46
Thasos: 42
threats, abusive: 66, 68-73
toponym, comic: 65 n.16
Tzetzes: 21

violence, verbal: 1, 15, 63-64, 66, 70, 73

wishes, malevolent: 65, 71-73

Xanthias: 15, 46

Zeus: 31; standing for Pericles in Cratinus: 55-57